AMERICA'S
NEXT
TWENTY

AMERICA'S NEXT
TWENTY YEARS

❮❮❮❮❮❮❮❮❮❮❮❮❯❯❯❯❯❯❯❯❯❯❯❯

AMERICA'S NEXT TWENTY YEARS

by PETER F. DRUCKER

HARPER & BROTHERS
PUBLISHERS   NEW YORK

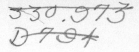

36943

AMERICA'S NEXT TWENTY YEARS

Library of Congress catalog card number: 57-7974

Contents

AMERICA'S NEXT TWENTY YEARS

⪻⪻⪻⪻⪻⪻⪻⪻⪻⪻⪻⪻⪼⪼⪼⪼⪼⪼⪼⪼⪼⪼⪼⪼

‹‹‹‹‹‹‹‹‹‹‹‹‹‹‹‹‹‹›››››››››››››››

CHAPTER ONE

The Coming
Labor Shortage

‹‹‹‹‹‹‹‹‹‹‹‹‹‹‹‹‹›››››››››››››››

THE MOST IMPORTANT economic event of the last few years has gone almost unreported in the newspapers. Few carried any announcement that well over four million babies have been born in this country every year since 1954 —the largest baby crops ever. Yet 1954, 1955 and 1956 should each have brought a record low in births rather than a record high. For the young women who reached marriageable age, married, and had their first child during these years were born, for the most part, in the dark depression years of 1933 and 1934, when the birth rate ran 30 or 40 per cent below the present figures. The number of marriages since 1954 has indeed been smaller than usual, but the total married population has had more than the usual number of children.

Between now and 1975 the number of young people reaching marriageable age will tend to increase. Since romance is reliably constant, this means an appreciable increase in the rate of family-formation and in the number of births to be expected each year. Six or eight years from now the birth figure should take another mighty leap upward as the children born in the years of the "baby boom" since 1942 begin to reach maturity and form families of their own.

What now appears to be true, therefore, is that the low birth rate of the depression decade was a freak. The higher birth rate which reasserted itself in the early forties now appears to be the normal rate at which the American people reproduce themselves. Only about ten years ago the Census Bureau, misled by the depression figures, predicted that the American population would become static within a few years and start to decline soon thereafter. It was this interpretation which underlay most of the talk about a mature economy that played such an important role in American public policy during the thirties and early forties. But now we can say with some certainty that nothing short of a tremendous catastrophe—that is, an atomic war—could possibly stop or even slow down the growth of the American population for the next twenty years.

The reason we can be so certain, of course, is that in reckoning the adult population for the next two decades we do not have to predict; we know. *The major events that determine the future have already happened—irrevocably.* Everybody who will reach marriageable age during the next eighteen or twenty years has by now been born. Everyone who will join the work force within the next eighteen or twenty years has by now been born. And so, obviously, has everyone who will retire. The economic population of the next twenty years—its numbers, its age and sex distribution—is not just predictable today; *it is already in being.*

This chapter examines some of the implications arising from the single stupendous fact of today's birth rate. As in any prophecy, there will presumably be some boners—but with a difference. Our forecasting is severely limited to those future happenings that are already under way. There is no need for crystal-gazing. We can find plenty to occupy us in what we *know* about America's next twenty years from events that have already occurred.

MORE JOBS THAN WORKERS

We start with a paradox: there are going to be more people, and hence more jobs, but not more people to fill the jobs. It is more than possible, in fact, that a continuing feature of the next two decades will be a labor shortage— and that the basic problem of the period will not be unemployment but inflation. Let's look at some of the figures which show why this is true.

The total population of the United States, now at 168 million, can be expected to top 190 million by 1965 and 220 million by 1975. These are conservative assumptions. They make full allowance for a continuing drop in the birth rate in the one major sector of the populace where it is still high, and still dropping: the Negro. They allow for several years of birth rates as low as those of the thirties. They hardly take into account at all the fact that ten years hence the number of young people old enough to start their own families will be very much larger than it is at present. And they do not make allowances for any growth in the size of families. If the three-child family again becomes the norm, of course, as against the present average of two-and-a-half, the growth of population will be much faster.

The *rate* of population growth which the figures anticipate is no larger than our rate of growth for the past fifty years, including the thirties. It is the rate of population growth which has prevailed in this country virtually since colonial days, and which has brought about the steady doubling of the American people every half century. But the *total* number of new Americans this rate will add to our population is now exceptionally large. It took forty years—from 1910 to 1950—for America to grow by 40 million people. Now it should take less than twenty years.

At the same time that the total population will grow very rapidly, however, the *working population* will grow very slowly, if at all. With total population increasing by 25 million, the number between twenty and sixty-five years of age (the bulk of our working population) will go up at the most by 5 million. In the group from twenty-five to forty-five—the one from which every employment manager in the country prefers to choose—there will actually be a slight shrinkage. On the other hand, there will be 5 million more people over sixty-five, and at least 16 million more under twenty, than there are today.

From 1965 on, total population and working population should be in better balance. Beginning in the early sixties, the large baby crops of the forties will reach maturity. Population of working age will thus increase by 12 million or so during the decade 1965-75. And assuming that there is a slight drop rather than an increase in the birth rate of the families these grown-up children form, the subsequent increase in total population and in working population will stand in the same ratio (five to two) in which they stand today.

EXPLOSION IN THE COLLEGES

But the size of the working population is not entirely determined by the number of people of working age. An important factor is the number who are not available for work because they are in school.

If the birth rate was the most important economic event of the last few years, the second most important was the steady increase in the number of full-time and part-time college students. This began with an increase of 10 per cent, to an all-time high of 2.5 million in 1954. Since then —in only two years—the figure has risen to 3 million or more. The increase in the birth rate was contrary to all expectations; the increase in the number of college students is nothing short of miraculous. Not only have an abnormally low number of young people reached college age during the past years (the delayed result of the lean thirties), but the veterans studying under the GI Bill have all but disappeared. Seven or eight years ago, three quarters of the male students in many undergraduate colleges were GIs; today the figure is down to 10 or 15 per cent, most of them in the older classes. Yet the 1954, 1955 and 1956 jumps were in the *freshman* class, which contained almost no GIs and was drawn from the smallest college manpower reservoir of the recent past or the foreseeable future.

It had long been clear that the mid-fifties would show whether there had been any real change in the educational habits of the country, or whether the GI Bill (and the attempt of many young veterans to make up for lost time) had just created a temporary bulge in college enrollment. A drop of one third during these years would have been mild; indeed, it would still have supported the conclusion that going to college was rapidly becoming the normal thing to do. That there has been an *increase* rather than drop is thus overwhelming proof that—far from being a freak—the jump in college enrollment is another new normal. The college enrollment figures now show exactly the same trend that high school enrollment showed after World War I, when a high school education first became normal throughout the country.

Twenty years from now, at least 7.5 million and perhaps as many as 12 million young people can be expected to attend colleges and universities. Therefore, even though they are of working age, they will not be available for full-time work. Such a projection is again a conservative one; 12 million college students will still be less than half the young Americans of college or university age. Yet within a similar period—from the early twenties to the early forties—the number of young people in high school increased from a little under 20 to close to 90 per cent.

Such a substantial gain in college enrollment would come

none too soon. For our problem is not the breeding of an "intellectual proletariat" for whom there will be no jobs, but a need for more trained and educated man- and woman-power than the country can possibly supply. Indeed, as we will see in a subsequent chapter, the technological revolution of Automation, already under way, requires a tremendous increase in the number of trained and educated people. Already the short supply of such people is *the major limiting factor* on the rapid growth of our economy and of our principal industries. We need not worry, therefore, about our ability to absorb these millions of college-trained people; we have to worry principally about increasing their number and quality fast enough.

The explosive growth of college enrollment will create many problems some of which will be discussed later in this book. It certainly raises the most serious questions of educational policy, curriculum, and educational standards. It makes me wonder whether the colleges, especially the independent liberal arts colleges, really know what they are doing in their fund-raising and other campaigns. If I were a college president I would not—as so many seem to be doing—lower educational standards in the belief that this is the way to draw more students. I would try instead to raise standards, so as to make my college known for the quality of its education and the toughness of its academic requirements. There will be students aplenty.

What concerns us here, however, is merely the impact of this development on the size of the working population. We can expect that there will be only 2 million more men

and women available for work in 1965 than there are today
—that is, an increase of 5 million of working age minus an
increase of 3 million in college attendance. And, of the
12 million who will be reaching working age between
1965 and 1975, 5 million may go to college rather than
straight to work, leaving a net increase for the second decade
of only 7 million.

Finally, the size of the working population must also be
adjusted for time at work. There can be little doubt that
total hours worked will continue to decline as a result of
longer vacations, more holidays, and a shorter work week.
The American people have made it thoroughly clear that
they have decided to take, in the form of greater leisure, a
big slice of any increase in productivity.

*Here, in summary, is the basic population structure
within which the American economy will function during
the next twenty years:*

There will be a population increase of one-fifth *in the
next ten years.*

But total population of working age will increase only
by one-tenth.

Population actually available for work will increase only
by 6 per cent.

And total hours worked by the whole economy in the
course of one year *may not increase at all.*

And in the next twenty years, total population will increase by at least two-fifths.

Population of working age, however, will increase by less
than one-third.

Labor force will go up by one-fifth, and total hours worked by 10 per cent.

And even more intensive employment, on a larger scale, of older people who are willing and able to work—however desirable in itself—would not materially affect these conclusions.

These statements define a trend exactly opposite to that which dominated the twenties and thirties. Then, partly as a result of the drop in the birth rate and partly because of the cutting off of immigration, the population of working age tended to grow faster than the total population. We face the exact opposite, in other words, of the basic assumptions that underlay Keynesian economics; and the basic problem of economic policy in the two decades ahead should therefore not be unemployment but inflation.

A DIFFERENT KIND OF DEPRESSION

The supply of people to do the work, and of hours to do it in, will in fact be so short as to make any prolonged period of large-scale national unemployment highly improbable. This does not mean that we shall have no depression, or even that a depression is unlikely (though the constant new demands created by a rapidly growing population can be expected to act as a substantial cushion). It also does not mean that there may be no serious and chronic unemployment in any one industry, or in one area dependent on a decaying industry—as there is today in the Pennsylvania anthracite fields. But though depressions —even serious ones—may well happen, depression unemployment of the kind that characterized the thirties is unlikely.

Lest this be considered incongruous, if not silly—for we have come to consider the two words "depression" and "unemployment" as interchangeable—let me refer only to Soviet Russia, where for the past thirty years there have been violent and extreme economic fluctuations without unemployment; and where, though for entirely different reasons, there has been a labor shortage much like the one we are about to experience. What form such a depression-without-unemployment might take may be suggested by our experience from 1946 to 1949, when the three quarters of the working population who were not unionized (and were therefore not protected against inflationary price increases) suffered a cut in their real purchasing power fully comparable to the impact of a severe and prolonged depression. Even with high employment, inflation could have the same kind of destructive effect over the next twenty years.

Now, there is only one effective way to control long-range inflationary pressures, and that is increased productivity. Certainly it is the only way to convert inflation from a serious threat of economic and social disruption into an opportunity for economic and social advance. As one of several consequences of the population revolution, therefore, *increased productivity* will be the paramount need of the American economy in the decades ahead.

Mr. Ralph J. Cordiner, the president of General Electric, announced at the end of 1954 that by 1965 his company would have to produce and sell twice the volume of goods it had turned out that year with only 11 per cent more people on its payroll. Adjusted for the expected decrease in working hours, this means that eight years hence General Electric must be able to produce twice as much as in 1954 for every hour its employees work.

This is a sharper increase in both production and productivity than the over-all economy will have to show, for the electrical industry is growing a good deal faster than the national average. But even for an industry that grows only as fast as the nation at large, the increase ahead will have to be tremendous. A company that intends to maintain its competitive position in its own industry will have to be able, ten years from now, to produce two fifths more than it does today without much, if any, increase in its hours worked. Twenty years hence it will have to be able to turn out twice as much with only one-tenth more hours of work.

Put it in another way. Today every American at work supports himself (or herself) and one-and-a-half other people besides. Twenty years from now every American at work should produce enough to support, at today's standard of living, himself and three-and-a-half other people. And he will have to do this in fewer working hours.

This assumes, moreover, that the standard of living will only go up at the same rate it has been advancing for the past twenty-five years, half of which were years of depression and war. To achieve this—hardly an ambitious goal—productivity will, however, have to increase 40 per cent in the next ten years; it will have to be almost doubled in the next twenty years.

Despite all the emphasis we have given to productivity in recent years, we really know very little about it—and we certainly do not know how to measure it. But even if we take the most optimistic of the various guesses about the rise in productivity in the past few years—a guess that puts the net annual increase above 3 per cent—we are going to have to step up the rate considerably to make possible increased growth.

PAYING FOR PRODUCTIVITY

The first requirement is capital. We may not know much, but we do know that an increase in capital investment and an increase in productivity are tied together; and the higher the capital per worker the higher the productivity—and, incidentally the wages and salaries paid.

By 1955 we were spending $40 billion a year on capital investment. A good many economists consider even this tremendous sum to be too low; they feel that we have not yet made adequate allowance for the inflation of the forties, and they point to the fact that a good many businesses (especially the small ones) still base their provision for future new equipment on the deflated prices that prevailed in the thirties. These economists feel that in three major areas of the national economy we have an over-age plant which needs more capital investment than it gets: in housing, in transportation, and above all in education. They feel, too, that in many industries the machinery is rapidly wearing out and that American equipment, far from being modern, might well—in important respects—be on the verge of obsolescence.

But let us assume that $40 billion in capital investment are adequate for the needs of the 1957 economy. We would then need $65 billion a year in 1965 and at least $100 billion twenty years from now. To obtain such gigantic sums would not be easy under the best of circumstances. To make matters worse, as a later chapter will point out, the large investment trusts and pension funds are currently emerging as the country's only real "capitalists"; and this development by no means encourages the supply of that kind of capital.

But there is another and more important question: can the nation afford investment at such a rate? Today eleven cents out of every dollar produced in this country is put back into capital for the future. To obtain an adequate amount in 1975, however, we would have to put back fifteen cents out of every dollar. Eleven cents is already high—higher than we have ever plowed back except in wartime. Fifteen cents may be wholly impossible, except under such stringent government control of interest rates or installment buying as would be considered unbearable —and rightly so.

We must, if this is the case, find ways to obtain more productivity for our investment dollar than we do today. If new investment is to be kept at or below 10 per cent of national product, we must learn by 1965 to get as much additional productivity out of $55 billion per year as we now would get out of $65 billion—as much, in 1975, out of $70 billion as we now would get out of a $100 billion. We must, in other words, increase the productivity of capital itself by one sixth by 1965 and by one third during the next twenty years.

This is not a new problem, to be sure. Economic progress might even be defined as the process of continually obtaining more productivity for less money. The means to achieve this is *innovation*. Without constant innovation, that is, all the capital invested in this country since 1750 might have been barely enough to permit the present population to live at a 1750 scale of living; the entire improvement in living standards since then is the result of innovation. Innovation has been the real "frontier" of the Western world these past two centuries. And what now distinguishes an "underdeveloped country"—and *keeps* it underdeveloped—is not so much a shortage of capital as it is shortage of innovation.

THE CHALLENGE TO INNOVATE

To the layman—and the typical businessman—"innovation" means "research" or "engineering," new products or new productive processes. These are indeed important aspects of innovation; and the four-fold increase (from $1 billion in 1950 to $4 billion in 1955) in the sums spent by American business on research and engineering for new products and new processes is therefore a highly encouraging sign. We already know that the next twenty years will bring about major changes in manufacturing, amounting to a technological revolution. And we also know that in a major industry like housing we badly need both radically new products and much more efficient production. But it is a serious mistake to think of innovation exclusively as technological innovation. The most important area of innovation—and the most productive one—may well be the opposite of technological.

During the past ten or fifteen years, the innovations that have had a major impact on the American economy were nearly all non-technological, were nearly all innovations in something else than product or process. First among them stand the tremendous changes in distribution methods. Hardly less important, especially in its impact on productivity, has been the development of new concepts of business organization. There have been tremendous innovations in plant, store, and office architecture; similarly in respect to the management of worker and work, whether industrial engineering, human relations, or personnel management. Finally there is the emergence of new basic management tools, especially measurements and controls like budgets, cost accounting, production scheduling, and inventory controls.

Among the major innovations of the past ten or fifteen years, only one can even remotely be called an innovation in product or productive process. That is the development of systematic and organized methods of materials handling. Otherwise, in their aggregate, the basically non-technological innovations have had a greater impact on the American economy, and have contributed more to the increase in productivity in this country, than all technological innovations of the past ten or fifteen years. In the long view of history, it is for social inventions—and not technical ones —that Americans may be best remembered.

During the period ahead, in any event, the greatest need for innovation seems more likely to lie in the social than in the technological area. Indeed, the technological revolution itself will be totally unproductive unless it is accompanied by major innovations in the non-technological field. Among them, above all, is again innovation in marketing. Equally badly needed are innovations in methods, tools, and measurements for doing the managerial job in the modern enterprise, large or small; for the development of competence, skill, and imagination among managers (still considered a luxury by many companies) is probably the greatest necessity any business, let alone the economy, faces. Finally, the need is for effective innovation in the management of workers and in the organization of work; despite the progress in this area, it may well be the most backward sphere, and the one with the greatest potential for increased productivity.

Compared to electronics, rocket engines, or synthetic chemistry, these are unglamorous subjects. They are rarely discussed except by professional managers, and not as often as they should be, even so. Yet our success at innovating in these four areas may well decide whether the population revolution, which has already taken place, will be an opportunity for further growth and strength, or whether it will prove a strain, a burden, and perhaps even a threat to social and economic stability.

CHAPTER TWO

The Promise
of Automation

IN HIS PRESIDENTIAL address to the annual convention of the CIO in 1954, Walter Reuther introduced an ungainly technical term into the headlines. He spoke of the coming "Automation Revolution." Automation, Reuther declared, is not in the future; it is already here.

Though the general public had not heard a great deal of Automation before, Reuther of course was not the first to interest himself in either the word or the thing it stands for. The word was coined at least a decade before—by Del Harder, Ford's manufacturing vice-president—and despite its ugliness it is now firmly established in the business language. For the past five or six years, in fact, Automation has become one of the most popular subjects of discussion at management association meetings; whole three-day sessions are sometimes devoted to this single topic. Two flourishing technical magazines deal with nothing else, in addition to a substantial number of books.

There can be no doubt that Reuther was entirely right

in his main assertion: Automation is not just in the future; it is here. And there is just as little doubt that it represents a major economic and technological change, a change as great as Henry Ford ushered in with the first mass production plant fifty years ago. Automation is the technological revolution of the second half of the twentieth century, just as mass production was of the first half. Its impact may be equally great, and may come faster.

Examples of Automation at work abound. A modern oil refinery is a pretty good one; and so is the pipeline system through which crude oil flows from Texas, guided by electronic impulses sent out all over the country from one control center. The way checks are cleared today in one of the big New York banks is a good example, too; and so is the system by which large insurance companies send out premium notices to millions of policyholders. A telephone dial exchange is another example; and so is the machine that registers the time of a long-distance call, computes the cost, and puts the amount on the customer's bill. Ford has an engine factory in Cleveland which comes very close to Automation; and the Sears Roebuck mail order plants, though there is very little machinery in them, are organized on a system which remarkably resembles Automation.

What do all these highly different applications have in common? What makes them examples of Automation? How can the term be defined?

Automation can be defined simply though superficially as the use of machines to run machines. We use machines today primarily to *do* things to material; to cut it, to sew it, to heat it or to cool it, to mix it, or to separate it. But for machines to be able to perform these functions four things must be done to help them. First, material must be moved—to the machine, in the machine, from the machine. Second, keeping the machine doing its job requires a lot of routine judgments: Is the tool getting too hot? Is the speed right? Do the pieces come out the way they should? Third, the setting of the machine (and the tools in it) has to be changed every so often—in most production jobs, very often. Usually the machine has to be stopped to do this, has to be opened or partially dismantled and then put together again, all by hand. Fourth, and finally, we need a lot of information to keep the machines running— the number of pieces it turns out, what kind of pieces, how fast, how many of them are faulty, and so forth. This information has to be gathered together somewhere, to be interpreted, and to be passed on to other people.

On the whole, astonishingly little attention has been given by engineers and production men to these four jobs. Yet we have known for a long time that they cost more than the actual fabricating done by the machines. They take more people and more time; in a typical metal-working plant, for every hour the machine works, at least five, sometimes even ten, man-hours have to be spent on them; and they account for practically all the employment on the production floor of a modern plant. Hence the importance of Automation, for in essence it means that these four jobs of (1) materials handling, (2) routine judgment, (3) machine setting, and (4) data processing, are done by machines instead of by hand—in a fraction of the time and at a very much lower cost.

As Mr. Reuther said, this is no longer in the future. For some time it has been possible to mechanize *any one* of these jobs. Mechanical machine setting, for instance, is as old as Jacquard's automatic loom, all of a hundred and fifty years. What had hitherto been lacking was primarily awareness of the size, cost, and importance of running and controlling machines. Once these appeared—largely as a result of World War II experience—Automation was here, full fledged. All that remained was the purely technical job of designing instruments, and that is being tackled with speed and energy.

HOW TO GO BANKRUPT

So far this all sounds like a job largely for engineers and tool designers. That is the way it is often tackled—a sort of push-button performance that puts men out of work. The "automatic factory" and an "automated business" are assumed to be almost the same thing.

But they are nothing of the kind. To try to build an automatic factory in a business that has not otherwise been automated is like trying to put a 1957 Turbojet aircraft engine into a 1913 Ford Model T. The business could not use the power that the automatic factory delivered; it would be impossible to connect one with the other; and, even if it weren't, the automatic factory would literally shake the business to pieces. To put automatic factories into a business that has not first been automated in other respects may well bankrupt it; at the least, they will saddle it with risks and costs beyond any benefit they can possibly produce.

The automatic factory is the end product rather than the beginning of Automation. Automation properly does not start with production at all, but with an analysis of the business and its re-design on Automation principles. The form that automatic production takes in the plant is determined by that analysis and re-design; and mechanization, the replacement of human labor by machines, is a detail of Automation and not always the essential one. The reason for this, the reason why Automation has to be business-focused rather than production-focused, is that it radically shifts the area of *business risk*.

CREATING THE MARKET

In the traditional systems of production the major risk, that of economic fluctuation, is absorbed by production. Production is cut down when business falls off; it is stepped up when business improves. Our entire economic theory, as far as it goes, is based on this risk-absorbing function of production. Under Automation, however, production can no longer absorb the risk of economic fluctuations.

Automation requires continuous production at a set level of output for a considerable period of time—three months, six months, maybe a year. This means that short-term adjustments cannot normally be taken care of by changing production schedules except at exorbitant cost. In fact, under Automation it may no longer make much sense to speak of "cost per unit of production." A much more appropriate unit of cost may be "cost per time of production at a given capacity rate," which is the cost concept of our most nearly automated industry, petroleum.

One illustration of the marketing system developed, of necessity, by the petroleum industry is the old story of John D. Rockefeller's giving away kerosene lamps to the Chinese coolies, to establish an assured demand for his products. For Automation, as an absolute first condition, requires the establishment of a fairly predictable, stable, and expanding market. For example, to apply Automation to the manufacture of kitchen appliances such as ranges, dishwashers, and automatic washing machines would require an organized market for second-hand appliances. It might even be necessary for the manufacturer to stop selling appliances entirely and instead sell the housewife a five-year service policy, with the appliances on loan or at a nominal rent; at the end of five years the appliances would then be replaced by new ones—thus making possible a predictable production schedule. Nor is this idea as outlandish as it sounds: a study made for one appliance company concluded that the service contract would work if only a manufacturer existed who knew how to make good on it.

Automation requires that management find out the basic facts about its business, the market for its products, its demand expectations, the variations between different products and different product lines. It requires hard work on product planning, pricing, product design, and product service. Indeed Automation in many cases requires a complete re-thinking of the product. It requires deliberate planning for technological change—that is, directed efforts to make products systematically obsolete by bringing out better ones on a pre-set schedule. It requires new concepts and new methods of information and measurement. And it requires exceptionally clear thinking about the design and structure of the entire business—its goals, its environment, its resources, and its organization.

WHAT MAKES IT WORK

There are three basic principles which make up the logic of Automation. Wherever the three are actually used there is genuine Automation even if there are no automatic machines, no electronic controls or computers, no mechanical brains. Unless all three principles are understood and consciously applied, Automation will not work.

The first of these is the principle of *economic activity as a process*. In early industry, as typified by the job shop, the integrating principle of work was skill. In Henry Ford's concept of mass production the organizing principle was the product. In Automation, however, the entire activity of the business is a whole entity which must be harmoniously integrated to perform at all.

A process knows neither beginning nor end. It may have stages but it does not divide into parts as such. From the ultimate consumer back to the first supplier of raw materials it has to be seamless, so to speak, yet at the same time conform to the second principle: that of *pattern, order, or form* behind the seemingly random and unpredictable flux of economic phenomena. If a business is to be considered a continuous process, instead of a series of disjointed stop-and-go events, then the economic universe in which a business operates—and all the major events within it—must have rhyme, rhythm, or reason.

Without this underlying structure of forms in the economic universe, Automation would be both inconceivable and incapable of achievement. Such patterns apply to events of all kinds. They might be found in the rate and distribution of incoming orders. They might have to do with the "mix" in the demand for different products at different times. They might concern the speed with which the market becomes ready for new products. They might relate to personnel problems such as absenteeism, sickness, turnover, or employee performance. Even changes which appear unpredictable, such as changes in fashion, should be found to follow a clear (perhaps even a strict) pattern if properly analyzed.

Finally Automation has a principle of *self-regulating control* which derives from its nature as process. As every true process must, it contains the means of its own regulation and correction. It must be able to maintain the equilibrium between ends and means, output and effort. And it must be able ahead of time to set standards of acceptable performance, which it then can use as pre-tests and as governors. In electronics this is called "feed-back"—that is, a control in which the process, by its own product, regulates itself. The businessman has of course long been familiar with one such control: profit—the simple, though crude, device that uses the results of economic activity to control its future direction and the quantity of new resources devoted to it.

In these basic principles, Automation is little more than a projection into the economic sphere of philosophical beliefs that have become dominant in the past fifty years. The idea is distinctly characteristic of the twentieth-century thought that a diversity of patterns, processes, or forms— each capable of logical expression, logical analysis, and systematic synthesis—underlies all phenomena. It is the common contribution of the founding fathers of modern scientific philosophy like Poincaré, Bohr, and Planck; Willard Gibbs, Mendel, Hunt, and Malinowski. It was clearly understood by Henry Adams. It might, with considerable over-simplification, be calld an "organic" philosophy—if only to distinguish it from the strictly mechanistic approach on which Henry Ford's concept of mass production was based.

It is of course not necessary for a business manager to know anything about the philosophical foundations of Automation, let alone to be a philosopher or scientist himself. It is not even necessary for the experts in Automation within a business to know these things. But it is absolutely necessary for both the businessman and his Automation specialists to understand clearly that Automation is not a box of tricks or a bagful of gadgets. Automation is a methodology, with all the strengths and limitations that the term implies.

THE IMPACT OF A METHOD

If Automation were a simple matter of technology, or replacement of human labor by machines, its social impact would be precisely what Walter Reuther predicted: large-scale displacement of workers. It might still be arguable whether this displacement would result in mass unemployment, as Reuther said; the fact that during the next twenty years our working population will grow but slowly makes it implausible that there will be chronic unemployment, even if Automation comes very fast. Still, as long as Automation is seen as a mere matter of technology, displacement of workers would be the thing to worry about. But considered in its larger dimensions, as we have been considering it here, Automation's most important impact will not be on employment but on the qualifications and functions of employees.

There may actually be no workers on the production floor of tomorrow's push-button factory. There are practically none today in a power-generating station or an oil refinery. But at the same time incredibly large numbers of men will be required behind the scenes in new, highly skilled jobs as machine builders, machine installers, repair men, controllers of the machinery and of its performance, and as "programmers" to prepare and feed information into the machine. In addition, large numbers of highly educated men will be needed in new jobs as designers of machinery, draftsmen, system engineers, mathematicians, or logicians. Finally, large numbers will be needed for new managerial jobs requiring a high ability to think, to analyze, to make decisions, and to assume risks. And this increase both in the numbers of managers and in the demands made on them may well be the largest of all the social impacts of Automation.

MACHINES AND MASTERS

Many people seem to fear that Automation will downgrade the worker by making him a slave to a mechanical monster. "I have charge of one of the large electronic computers," a young engineer said to me a few months ago. "I am constantly appalled by the number of people who seem to think that the machine has charge of me."

One look at the industries that are virtually automated now, such as electric power generation or oil refining, should show that they have plenty of employees, that they pay the highest wages, and that there is little room in them for unskilled or untrained labor.

Mass production upgraded the unskilled laborer of yesterday into the semi-skilled machine operator of today—and in the process multiplied both his productivity and his income. In just the same way, Automation will upgrade the semi-skilled machine operator of today into a highly skilled and knowledgeable technician—multiplying his income again. Norbert Wiener, MIT's distinguished mathematician, who did much of the conceptual thinking that underlies the new technology, has predicted that Automation will lead to "the human use of human beings"—that is, to our using man's specifically human qualities, his ability to think, to analyze, balance and synthesize, to decide and to act purposefully—instead of using him, as we have done for millennia, to do all the dreary work machines can do better.

There are two reservations to the prediction that Automation will not cause large-scale labor displacement. First, Automation will mean a sharp cut in employment for routine office work. There machines will indeed replace men and women. But this, in total numbers, is not a major segment of the working population; it is largely composed of young, unmarried girls fresh out of school, who are in short supply today and will remain so for at least ten years. This has always been a labor force with a very high turn-over, where it will therefore be possible to introduce Automation without laying off people—all that is needed is to replace at a progressively slower rate the employees who quit.

The second reservation is that Automation will involve a considerable shifting of men to new jobs with new employers. For instance, there will be a tremendous demand for men to build machinery and equipment, but this demand may not arise for them in the same company that employs them now. Thus there may be considerable dislocation unemployment in a particular industry, and it may extend to a whole area that one industry dominates.

But the most important of these dislocations may well

be a shift of employment opportunities to *smaller* business. In the first place, Automation should strengthen the competitive position of the small company, if only because mechanical machine setting enables the small organization to offer a more complete and diversified range of products at a competitive cost. Secondly, Automation will create opportunities for countless small businesses to specialize in servicing equipment. One indication of the growth we can expect is shown by the small but highly expert tool-and-die makers who serve the automotive industry; it is an open secret in Detroit that these small shops make a higher percentage profit on their capital and enjoy greater stability than General Motors.

Socially, the shift in job opportunities therefore should be healthy. But it will still impose on management a responsibility to plan systematically for the retraining and placement of workers during the shift to Automation. Union leaders, too, should similarly accept responsibility for the changes in their rules that will be necessary. Even such sacred cows as seniority or apprenticeship restrictions may have to be slaughtered. It is a good sign that some managements—notably General Electric—and some unions —notably Reuther's United Auto Workers—are already at work on these matters.

The really serious social problem is not employment but the need to upgrade whole segments of the population in very short time. Automation requires trained and educated people in unprecedented numbers. The quantitative need alone will be so great that the 8 or 10 million college students we can expect fifteen years hence will be barely sufficient. One large manufacturing company (now employing 150,000) figures that it will need *seven thousand* college graduates a year, once it is automated, just to keep going; today it hires three hundred annually.

But the need is above all qualitative—for *better educated* people. The "trained barbarian," the man who has acquired high gadgeteering skill, will not do. Even in routine jobs, Automation will require ability to think, a trained imagination, and good judgment, plus some skill in logical methods, some mathematical understanding, and some ability well above the elementary level to read and write—in a word, the normal equipment of educated people. Under Automation, a school could do a student no greater disservice than to prepare him, as so many do today, for his first job. If there is one thing certain under Automation it is that the job—even the bottom job—will change radically and often.

NEEDED: EDUCATED MANAGERS

The greatest educational need may well be in management. Of course there will always be need for intuition, hunch, and experience in business enterprise, at least as long as we eschew state planning. But in an automated business the intuitive manager is obsolete; and experience under Automation will not be a very reliable guide. To be a manager in an automated business, of course, a man need not have a formal education, let alone a degree; indeed it would be hard to find an institution of learning where he could acquire today the education he needs to be a manager tomorrow. But, in the sense of being able to handle systematic knowledge, he will have to be *highly* educated.

This educational job will have to be done, to a large extent, in and by the business itself; and large companies in particular will have to become educational institutions —and interest themselves in formal education—even more than they do today. For the foreseeable future, there will simply not be enough new people with the new knowledge and skill required to fill the new jobs; and this will be true in all areas of the organization: rank and file, office work, technical and professional work, managerial work. On every level, adult education—largely on the job—will be needed.

THE NEW STABILITY

In any case, whatever dislocation Automation produces will take place in the period of transition from the old to the new, and it will be temporary. Permanently, Automation should introduce a new stability into the economic society. For Automation will have to stabilize the two factors which have hitherto both caused and suffered the greatest instability: capital investment and employment.

Piecemeal capital investment—to replace a machine here, to make an operation more efficient there—is simply not possible under Automation. Nor is it possible to make capital expenditure entirely dependent on cash income and business conditions, lopping them off as soon as sales or prices fall and hectically pushing them up in good times. The whole plant, under Automation, must be conceived as one integrated piece of machinery. No one part can be replaced, improved, or changed without changing the entire plant and all its parts; and once a capital project has been started it has to be carried through, on a timetable pretty well fixed in advance. If the project is abandoned midway, the sums already invested may be lost entirely.

This obviously creates new and serious risks. Obviously it will raise still higher the demands on management's ability to make long-range decisions. But at the same time it also means that a sizable portion of our capital spending will increasingly be carried out independently of the business cycle, and this in turn will stabilize the cycle. It will hardly eliminate economic fluctuations altogether, but it should prevent the extremes of boom and bust.

Probably we are already feeling these effects. Both the "inventory recession" of 1951 and the recession of 1954 were expected by the great majority of businessmen to turn into long, hard downswings. Yet few businesses stopped their capital expenditures programs: few even cut them back. The reason they gave for this totally unprecedented behavior was that capital investment programs are integrated and long-term and can hardly be adapted, once they have been begun, even to major cyclical fluctuations. As a result, neither recession went very far.

Automation should bring even greater stability to employment. In this area lies one of its greatest opportunities. Management today still proceeds on the assumption that labor is a current expense which fluctuates, on the whole, with volume of production. Already this concept may be obsolete; in most large companies one third or more of the employees are salaried; and of the hourly employees, a half or even two thirds, in many industries, have to be kept on the job as long as the plant is open, regardless of output.

Under Automation, however, the traditional concept will be untenable, if not dangerous. Labor under Automation must be considered a capital resource, with wage costs being treated virtually as fixed costs. The essence of Automation is its inability to adjust production to short-range economic fluctuations, except within narrow ranges. The number of people employed will therefore not fluctuate directly with volume, and the investment in the skill and training of workers will be much too great for the enterprise to disperse them, except in a situation of extreme peril.

Automation thus creates the opportunity for a high degree of employment stability—an opportunity that comes none too soon, since the social pressure for such stability has long been building up. This is partly a result of the American economy's success in making the worker "middle class"; the most potent emotional symbol of middle-class status has always been the salary in contrast to the wage. In part it is also the result of the disproportion between the rapid increase in total population and the slower increase in working population, and of the resulting labor pressure. But, in any case, the demands for stabilized employment and predictable income are certainly not inventions of the "power-hungry union bosses." They are the most important goals of the American worker.

HOW FAST WILL IT COME?

The Automation Revolution is here, and it is proceeding at high speed. But it will be many years before it permeates the entire economy. Most businesses will not convert to Automation overnight but will go at it piecemeal, which will not be easy. It will require more capital than wholesale Automation, and it will entail greater risks. But the mental strain will be less. Fewer people will have to relearn fewer things; and they will have more time to do it in. While it is a major revolution, Automation is therefore not likely to be dramatic; there will be no point when one can say: "This is the year when the American economy went into Automation."

But only the speed of Automation is uncertain. There can be little doubt that the direction of our progress is toward it. There can be little doubt that it means a tremendous upgrading of the labor force in terms of skill, employment security, standard of living, and opportunity. Above all, there can be little doubt that Automation is not technocracy under another name and that the push-button factory is not its symbol. Automation is not gadgeteering, it is not even engineering; it is a concept of the structure and order of economic life, the design of its basic patterns integrated into a harmonious, balanced, and organic whole.

CHAPTER THREE

The New

Tycoons

THERE ARE SOME one thousand companies listed on the New York Stock Exchange. In about one quarter of these, members of the founding family or of the present management own effective control. In the great majority, however, the only large stockholders are institutional trustees for other people's money: investment trusts, pension funds, and banks. Together these fiduciary investors have effective working control of these companies—that is, of the commanding position in our economy. Their holdings amount to almost one third of all the marketable common shares of American business.

By and large, these enormous holdings have been acquired in the past ten years. The pension funds only got going after World War II; there were about two thousand then, there are twenty thousand now. Ten years ago both investment trusts and bank-managed personal trusts were still insignificant. The shift of the center of security buy-

ing since then represents an unprecedented democratization of business ownership, for the real owners of these
holdings are small people, the middle class and the workers. It also represents an unprecedented concentration of
legal ownership, for the number of fiduciary managers is
fairly small.

Despite its speed and importance, this shift has had
amazingly little public attention. When General Motors
set up its pension fund nine years ago, it hired Clarence
Stanley—then a partner of Morgan, Stanley & Co., the
country's most powerful investment bankers—to manage
the fund. There could be no more perfect example of the
"capitalist revolution" than this move of J. P. Morgan's
direct successor from heading the very symbol of Wall
Street to managing the savings of "proletarians"—especially since it was quite obvious that Mr. Stanley was both
bettering himself financially and acquiring much more
financial power. Yet no new Horatio Alger rose to tell
this twentieth-century version of "From Rags to Riches."
It was noted, if at all, only in a few financial pages.

Anonymity, however, is exactly what our new masters
prefer. The fiduciary managers are as unlike the old Lords
of Creation as they could possibly be. They run heavily to
Ph.D. degrees and Phi Beta Kappa keys. Their incomes
generally are modest, usually much less than those of ex-
ecutives in the companies whose stock they manage.
Rather than buy yachts, they build up good economic
and statistical libraries. If any of them felt like playing
the stock market for his own benefit, one or another gov-

ernment agency—the Securities Exchange Commission, the State Insurance Commissioners, or the Banking Inspectors—would have him thrown out in short order. And not one of them would ever dream of entertaining the chorus of a musical comedy—not even at the Automat. They are certainly the soberest, least conspicuous, and most studious of all of our managerial groups.

It is unlikely that the public at large has even heard the names of men like Clarance Stanley of GM, Wallace Dunkel of the Bankers Trust Company's pension fund department, or Merrill Griswold of Massachusetts Investors Trust. Even in the financial community they are barely known; when the Fulbright Committee investigated the stock market in 1955 none of them was called to testify. Yet they are the "New Tycoons." In financial importance and the impact of their decisions on the economy, they—and the other managers of large investors—represent more power than the tycoons of yesteryear ever dreamed of possessing. They could easily match resources with a Rockefeller or a Carnegie, the most lordly of the "old" tycoons whose names are still, half a century after their heyday, household words throughout the world. The Sears Roebuck pension fund owns 26 per cent of the stock of the world's largest merchandising business; The General Motors pension fund has almost $100 million of new money to invest every year; and the Massachusetts Investors Trust, largest of them all, has a "cool billion" in assets.

Even the small fry among them carry a lot of financial

weight. The pension fund of the Owens-Illinois Glass Company, for instance, owns the biggest office building in Toledo, Ohio; the glass company itself is among its tenants. And the power and wealth of the New Tycoons is likely to grow still greater. Pension funds still cover little more than a sixth of American workers. A new push by the unions or fairly minor changes in the tax laws might at any time release a new tidal wave of pension fund formation like that of the past few years.

WHERE THE MONEY GOES

The democratization of business ownership by the fiduciary investor is an achievement without parallel in economic or social history, but it is also a perplexing one. Indeed, the very things that made it possible are problematic. Our economy has made the small man the major supplier of capital—but does enough of it go where it is needed to maintain a growing economy? We have created appropriate institutions to manage the small man's resources—but do they put an adequate share of their venture capital into new or small business?

The fiduciary investors among them own about $40 billion worth of common stock. Since this is a prodigious amount, it may at first seem absurd to ask whether it is enough. But the fiduciary investors have become practically the only source of new common stock capital. The New York Stock Exchange estimates that for every dollar of new money they spend on buying common stock, only five cents are invested directly by private investors—and this in a period of rapidly rising stock market prices. The pension funds alone receive each year a full third of all the savings the American people can afford to set aside for new investment. Yet only a fraction of the new money amassed each year by the fiduciary investors goes into common shares. All told, the fiduciary trustees have available for investment each year about $9 billion. Of this only $1.5 billion, at the most, is invested in common stock.

This is far too little for the needs of the economy. The amount of common stock capital available largely dictates the amount of innovation and expansion business will undertake. Such activities are rightly financed by equity capital—that is, primarily by common stock—rather than by borrowing. There is of course a second source of capital for such investments in the profits companies retain rather than pay out as dividends. But even if liberal allowance is made for this, the total amount available on the capital market for innovation and expansion is still too low. We now invest capital at the rate of $40 billion a year but will have to step up this rate considerably. Surely we need to put a larger share than 4 per cent into venture capital.

There are, in fact, clear signs that the economy already is inadequately nourished with venture capital. One clue is the extent to which expansion and innovation has come to depend on profits retained and re-invested in the business. Since the end of World War II, such earnings furnished six or seven times as much venture capital as did the capital market. Only the large, well-established company can normally get capital for expansion and innovation from this source, however, for generally they are the only ones—especially under our present tax laws— with sufficient built-up earnings. They naturally invest in fields with which they are familiar; more promising areas of economic enterprise may have to go without.

Another symptom is the extent to which we now finance new ventures through fixed obligations liks bonds, mortgages, or bank loans. Practically all new retail stores, for instance, have been financed up to 100 per cent of cost by bank or insurance company loans. The lender may be adequately protected; it may be a safe investment for him; but the borrower is assuming burdens which an earlier generation of retail merchants would have looked upon with dismay. Traditionally, in a boom such as the one we have been experiencing, business cuts its fixed debts and replaces them with venture capital—that is, with common stock. This has been the first boom in our history during which fixed obligations have become a larger, and not a smaller, proportion of business capitalization. While our tax laws may have been even more responsible for this than the lack of venture capital, it is hardly a desirable development.

The classic argument against a "soak-the-rich" policy has been that only the rich can supply the venture capital an expanding economy needs. If the middle classes and the workers can save money at all, it is said, they invest in the past rather than in the future. (They tend to catch up with themselves, and get the things they previously could not afford, before they move ahead.) But an economy that cannot invest in the future is a dying economy. We are justly proud of having made the middle classes and working people capable of replacing the millionaire capitalist of old—but the ancient argument that these new capitalists cannot supply enough venture capital has still to be disproved. We have yet to discover how to channel an adequate part of the income of the New Tycoons into common stock.

FALSE CONSERVATISM

The key to this problem is in the hands of our oldest, largest, and most powerful fiduciary investors, the life insurance companies. With well over $80 billion in assets, they represent greater financial power than all the trusts and pension funds put together. They are also trustees for many more people—for 32 million (out of a total of 42 million) American families, who hold 115 million individual life insurance policies and group insurance contracts. To most of these families the insurance policy represents their largest, often their only, capital asset.

Yet the United States life insurance companies—and only those of the United States—own virtually no common stock. Two fifths of their assets are invested in the bonds of private companies. Almost one third is in mortgages. Total common stock holdings are barely $2 billion, or less than 3 per cent. There are not even common stocks

41

in the pension funds they manage. The banks that manage pension funds, however, put a third of their monies into common stock.

This policy has an honorable history, but it has long since lost whatever sense it used to make. To shun common stock investments is not in the interest of the insured individual; it is the opposite of conservative. The last depression showed that sound common stock is safer than the mortgages on office buildings, apartment houses, and homes which figure so prominently in the portfolios of life insurance companies—safer even than a good many railroad or industrial bonds.

The traditional policy is also far from advantageous to the life insurance companies. It may explain why they have lost ground in the postwar period and now attract a smaller share of total savings than they did before the war. Though the life insurance companies invented the pension fund, they get only a third of pension fund business, primarily because the customers demand adequate common stock investments. "A worker who has a pension," as one of the shrewdest managers of pension funds in this country points out, "does not expect a certain amount in dollars but a certain purchasing power, no matter how many dollars it takes to provide it."

And this means that pension funds, to be conservative, must carry a substantial amount of common stock as a hedge against inflation.

There is one real obstacle left to large-scale common

stock buying by life insurance companies: they have fixed liabilities to meet as soon as a claim arises. They therefore need fixed, or at least predictable, income. But common stock dividends fluctuate with earnings. If American industry follows the trend toward Automation, this obstacle will grow bigger. Since production and labor force have to be kept fairly constant under Automation, the full burden of adjustment to economic ups-and-downs will fall on profits. Common stock earnings will fluctuate even more than they have traditionally.

Yet there is a way out of the impasse. Over any calendar year business profits will indeed have to fluctuate. But over a longer time-span—three, five, in some businesses, ten years—they can be predicted and planned, as a good many companies (Armstrong Cork, General Motors, or the Telephone Company) have successfully proven over the past twenty-five years. At the same time, the institutional investors, too, can adjust by planning on a five-year rather than a one-year basis; or a business (tax laws permitting) might lay aside earnings in a good year to cover the dividend in a poor one.

In other words, though it will take better financial planning than we have ever been used to, the obstacle can be overcome. If the life-insurance companies invest one fifth of their new money in common stock, for the next ten years, at the end of the decade they will still have less than 10 per cent of their assets in common stock— surely not an extravagant proportion. But this would almost double the supply of venture capital to the capital market—and give us the base the economy needs to grow and to expand.

But what about the small and growing business? Practically without exception, the funds invested today in common stock go to the large, well-established companies. Only these companies can have their securities listed on the Stock Exchange; and unlisted securities do not attract the fiduciary investor. The life insurance companies, if and when they start to buy common stock, are certain to be even more concerned with the marketability of their holdings, and will be even more likely to channel their funds into the large and old company.

Of course, the fiduciary investors would be grossly remiss in their duty as trustees if they were to invest in any but marketable and listed common stock. But the danger is also obvious: it gives the big companies practically a monopoly on access to the means of growth. This may not represent a positive change for the worse, since the young business has always had difficulty obtaining equity capital. But it remains socially and economically undesirable that small and growing businesses should be limited, if not deprived, of access to the capital market.

A solution to this problem has been found by the Massachusetts Investors Trust in Boston. Together with several small fiduciary investors, it has founded a company specifically intended to supply equity capital for new ventures: the American Development and Research Corporation. This company is sufficiently large for its shares to be listed on the Stock Exchange; thus fiduciary trustees can invest substantial sums in it.

Here might be the pattern for combining responsibility to the individual beneficiary with responsibility to society. Ultimately we might have a number of development companies, some within one region, some within one industry, others (like American Development and Research) specializing in new technological processes, and so forth, Whatever the device, finding it is a major responsibility for the fiduciary manager, and one that deserves high priority.

WHO RUNS INDUSTRY?

Power and responsibility pose a final question—and the toughest one. It can be simply stated: should the fiduciary trustees, in whose hands the real financial power of this country increasingly lies, exercise the right to control the management of companies whose legal owners they are? Should they demand a place on the board of directors, appoint and remove management people, review and approve company decisions? Are they entitled to exercise this control even though they are only "legal" owners?

Or should they take the attitude, as trustees, that they are neither entitled to nor responsible for the management of business? They are investors, not entrepreneurs; and the money they have invested is not theirs anyhow. Should they religiously refrain from any control—perhaps even be forbidden, as some industrial managements contend, from ever voting the stock which is legally in their name?

These are obviously important questions. The answers will largely determine the structure of industrial society in the years to come. But when the first pension trust was started, forty or fifty years ago, these questions were scarcely considered. The Sears Roebuck profit-sharing fund, probably the most successful of all, was started in 1916. It blithely provided that the income of the fund should be invested in common stock of the company and that the officers of the company should vote the stock on behalf of the beneficiaries. But at that time, apparently, nobody foresaw that forty years later the pension fund would own 26 per cent of the company's stock and be the only large stockholder.

Today, on the other hand, the managements of fiduciary investors are so conscious of the power they could wield that they swing to the opposite extreme. In the charter of most new pension funds there is a provision forbidding purchase of the company's own stock. Many of the funds even forbid investment in the stock of competing companies. The charters also provide that only a fraction of the assets of the fund may ever be invested in any one company. They provide further that no more than a small fraction (5 to 10 per cent) of the capital of any one company may ever be purchased by the fund. And finally, by tacit consent, it is understood that the holdings of the funds will not be voted.

"Our interest is purely financial," the top man in one of the largest pension funds said to me. "We are not owners and we are not managers. If we do not like a company or its management, we sell the stock. We have neither right nor competence to control. We can only act as trustees, and it is quite clear that interference with management does not lie within the trust we have received."

The reasons for such self-restraint are good and compelling. Even if no one of the fiduciary investors owned more than 5 or 10 per cent of a company's stock, together they would dominate unless they voluntarily refrained from doing so. They would all normally tend to think and act alike; they are people with the same interests, the same training, and the same responsibilities. As for controlling the industry, it would really not make much difference whether there were one or twenty such fiduciary investors. By exercising their legal power, they would bring American industries under that most dubious of masters—control by the financial mind.

But how satisfactory is this alternative—that is, the system we have now? First, it is probably not good enough even to satisfy the present demands on the fiduciary by his principal, the individual investor. It is simply not true that the fiduciary institution can sell its shareholdings whenever it loses confidence in management. It owns so much that it can sell only to an equally large investor— that is, to another fiduciary, And is it really likely that there will be demand for a big chunk of stock on the part of other fiduciary investors just when one of them decides that he wants to get out of an investment—particularly stock in a company where the management is inadequate?

Precisely because they form the real capital market in this country today, the fiduciary investors cannot liquidate their holdings except slowly. Their one way of passing judgment on a company is so drastic that it is virtually unusable. Thus the presently accepted policy means that management is essentially responsible to no one. By their abstention from voting and control, in the majority of cases, the fiduciary institutions simply confirm the incumbent officers.

At the same time, hypothetically, as long as they openly abstain from voting their stock as a matter of policy, the dominant holders cannot save a competent management from being "blitzed." All unwittingly, they invite the attention of any financial sharpshooter or stock market manipulator who wants to get control of a firm in order to milk it. If 40 to 60 per cent of the company voting stock is in the hands of fiduciary investors who will not vote, then control of the company can be obtained by buying up on the Stock Exchange 5 to 15 per cent of the stock—a fairly small fraction. Then the raiding group can appeal to the scattered mass of small stockholders in a battle for proxies; and the company that has been careful in building up property, or in plowing back earnings for expansion and research, is peculiarly vulnerable to such blitzing tactics. Its management can all too easily be made to look as though it had withheld from the stockholder earnings that should have been paid out in dividends.

The fiduciary trustees are therefore caught in a genuine

conflict of responsibility between the duties they owe to the beneficiaries of their funds and the duties they owe to the country as guardians of its capital resources. They cannot be allowed to exercise the full legal ownership power they possess. But at the same time they cannot be absolved from their responsibility to make sure that the companies they own are managed professionally, competently, and with high standards of integrity. In other words, they are not just trustees of the individual saver or investor. They are also trustees of one of America's most critically important resources, which is the performance and vision of our organized economic institutions.

A NEW KIND OF ADVISER?

The present hands-off attitude is the right one for the time being. Until we know how the New Tycoons should discharge their responsibility, it is better for them to be modest, self-restrained, and strict constructionists of their legal right. But this cannot satisfy the needs of our society for the long pull; and while we do not have, as yet, any real solution, we do have some beginnings.

Some of the fiduciary investors, for example, are thinking of bringing in a number of independent and objective advisers on management. Some of these advisers would be distinguished industrialists; others, men in public or academic life. It would be their function to keep a watchful eye on the companies in which a fiduciary has a major investment, and to be in close touch with the management of these companies. These men—while appointed for a specific period of time, compensated adequately, and outside of the control of the management of the fiduciary institution itself—would have the responsibility for suggesting when the fiduciary should drop the purely passive and self-restrained role of the investor and assume a positive role as an owner, in which the legal rights of ownership and the voting power would be exercised.

Similarly, some of the large, publicly owned companies —conscious of the fact that ownership of their securities is coming to rest more and more in fiduciary-investor hands—are talking about the appointment to their own boards of directors of two or three men of similar standing. Their primary duty would be to establish liaison between the company and its major institutional owners, to advise management of the needs of the institutional holders and their beneficiaries, and in turn to keep the fiduciary institutions informed on the plans and decisions of management. This would mean in effect that the fiduciary investors, without themselves going on the board of a company, would have spokesmen and informants on the board to enable them better to judge when to act as if they were the real owners, and how.

But these are the barest of beginnings. This is a big job —much bigger, perhaps, than I have been able to indicate here. While it appears to be a matter of financial policy, the issue is in essence nothing less than the legitimacy of management in contemporary America—that is, a society in which management is increasingly professional and ownership is increasingly a mere title to income, held anonymously and scattered in almost sub-atomic particles.

This question of the legitimacy of management may well be the toughest yet to be answered by the modern industrial society. It is certainly a central one. In every other country the alternative to the tycoon of yesterday, the acquisitive robber baron, seems to have been government ownership. In this country we have found a different alternative, the democratization of ownership in which the real owners are increasingly the employees themselves, But, in accomplishing this, we are concentrating legal ownership of industry in the hands of a comparatively small number of fiduciary investors. To the problems thence arising, clearly the solution lies in the realization on the part of these New Tycoons—in the sharpest possible contrast to the tycoons of yesteryear—that they have responsibilities both to the individuals for whom they manage their funds and to the commonweal, whose basic capital resources will be increasingly entrusted to their care.

‹‹‹‹‹‹‹‹‹‹‹‹‹‹‹‹‹‹›››››››››››››››››

CHAPTER FOUR

Will the Colleges
Blow Their Tops?

‹‹‹‹‹‹‹‹‹‹‹‹‹‹‹‹‹‹›››››››››››››››››

IF YOU ARE a parent with two or three children, the chances are that you will "buy" up to $36,000 worth of college and university education—a full tenth or more of your lifetime earnings. Even if you are childless, you will still be stuck with a bill for other people's children— through taxes and contributions. The financing of higher education affects everybody's pocketbook. It is the central problem of American education, and there is a great deal more at stake than mere money and taxes.

The problem is a paradoxical one. We do not yet know how to pay for the higher education we have, let alone for the amount we must have a decade or two hence. Yet the greatest weakness of our present system is that it attempts to do "on the cheap" what can only be done by spending a great deal more money.

College education in the United States is rapidly becoming "geneneral" education. But in its economic foundation it is still predominantly "class" education for a small group of the wealthy or exceptionally able. Today we have 3 million students in colleges and universities. By 1975 the college population will be at least 7.5 and perhaps as many as 12 million—a little less than 50 per cent of the eligible age groups. The jump in high school graduates alone—20 per cent of the eligible age group a generation ago, over 80 per cent today—would make inevitable such an explosion in college enrollments. And even 12 million college and university students would hardly be adequate to supply the country's need for educated men and women twenty years hence.

It is fashionable in academic circles to hope that the explosion will not occur—or at least that one's own school will escape the blast. An individual college may perhaps be able to command the shock waves to pass around it, but this only means that others will get hit worse.

When, for instance, the University of California in Los Angeles tried to slow down the rate of expansion by raising admission standards, San Diego State College immediately began to grow twice as fast. When San Diego in turn raised its standards, other colleges in Southern California began to mushroom. And when they jacked up their standards, the wheel came full circle; enrollments in the new community colleges of the University of California—such as Riverside—shot up.

The fact is that colleges and universities have got to grow, and to grow they must have money. But even if they get the money, can they continue to be the kinds of institutions we are used to? For three hundred years we have experimented with more and more kinds of colleges and universities—with the residential principle deeply embedded in their traditions. Is this a luxury we can continue to afford, or will our universities have to become monstrous city day schools?

In almost every college it costs more to educate a student than the college charges him for tuition. Part of this cost is faculty salaries, part is capital investment in physical plant, part is administration. But it is not only these costs that are worrying educators. They are also concerned about the financial burden that families who want to send their children to college must carry.

Let's look at each of these aspects of the financial nightmare.

1. *The tuition deficit.* What it costs a college or university to educate a student varies tremendously from college to college, from department to department within the college, and even between age groups in the same department. Think, for example, how much more it costs to train a young man who majors in physics, with all the elaborate equipment he requires, than one who studies foreign languages. Think how much less it costs to educate a student who attends large lecture courses with standard true-and-false tests than one who sits in small classes of fifteen or in seminars. Conservative authorities, such as the National Merit Scholarship Corporation recently created by large grants from the Ford and Carnegie Foundations, estimate that the minimum gap between what the

student pays and what he costs the college is about equal to the charge for tuition. That is, about $600 per student.

With 3 million students in colleges and universities today, the tuition deficit runs to at least $1.18 billion a year. By 1975 it will amount to $5 billion at a minimum—even if faculty salaries should stay right where they are. But, of course, they won't.

2. *The cost of faculty.* The budget for faculty salaries is going to have to go up. Even if classes are much larger than they are today, and each instructor teaches more students, we are going to need by 1975 more than twice our present supply of college teachers. We now have 225,000, and we will need half a million. Where will they come from?

We will have to recruit practically all of that half million, for few of the present faculty will be left for the job twenty years hence. We are losing 10,000 of the present faculty each year through death, retirement, or resignation. Even if every qualified graduate with a higher degree were to go into teaching we would be seriously short of teachers; of the 50,000 or so men and women who get advanced degrees each year (44,000 masters and 5000 to 6000 doctors) the great majority are trained in professional schools, which do not, as a rule, prepare for a teaching career. Of those who are qualified—perhaps 12,000 or so each year—fewer and fewer actually become teachers; of this year's crop, at most 6000 will actually accept any kind of academic employment. Total faculty personnel is thus shrinking when it should be expanding, and college teachers—rather than water, petroleum, or uranium—may well become our scarcest and most critical resource.

The problem is not just one of money. In the last twenty years academic life has become much less attractive to young men and women, and other careers beckon them with increasing persuasiveness.

I talked recently to the dean of a major university which prides itself on its reputation for scholarship and academic freedom, and he told me about the tight situation his own assistant professors face. The typical assistant professor has a Ph.D. degree, is thirty-four years old and married, with two or three children. He spends twelve hours a week in the classroom, five hours in committee meetings, fifteen hours in conferences with students, preparing lectures, and correcting papers, and seven hours "voluntarily" advising on all kinds of university chores ranging from work for the Air Force to Ford Foundation projects—a total of thirty-nine hours a week of regular university work. To make enough to live on he has to teach summer school, and this cuts his vacation to four or five weeks a year.

This load does not seem intolerable, but he is expected also to be a "productive" scholar. He should, for example, contribute without extra pay one big chapter to a university-sponsored publication each year. He is under pressure to publish at least two learned papers, the subjects of which are often assigned to him by his senior professor. He is also expected to "have a book" every three years—

and more likely than not he has to pay to get it published. The subjects he teaches are assigned by the department, and so are the books he must use. He has to be a specialist, for there is nothing so suspect as a "man without a specialty." *He is on an annual contract and has no job security nor promise of severance pay.* Tenure exists only for full and associate professors; and his chance of becoming an associate is one in four and then not until he is forty.

To regain its attractions, academic life needs radically to improve working conditions for younger faculty. It needs to offer greater job security, systematic ways of creating promotional opportunities, decent personnel management, and, above all, less pressure for intellectual over-specialization.

But it also needs money.

This was brought home to me sharply last year when, in short order, six young men and women came to me and asked my help in finding jobs outside of teaching. Each one of these six was recognized as a "comer" by his own colleagues and by university authorities. Each one carried big and important teaching assignments and was known as a brilliant teacher. They worked in major universities with comparatively high pay scales. Each one of these six young people loved teaching and academic life, and reached the decision to leave only after months of internal struggle. Yet every one of them had come to the conclusion that he simply could not afford to go on teaching. And—this is the real moral of the story—I was able with but little effort to find for every one of the six a job in business, in journalism, or in industrial research. In every case the new jobs paid at least twice as much as the university had paid, and more than it could be expected to pay until another ten or fifteen years of teaching.

The entire salary level of the academic profession will have to be raised—and doubling it will barely be adequate. We are now paying about $800 million a year in faculty salaries. By 1975, assuming the same purchasing power of the dollar, we will have to pay twice as much to more than twice as many people—or about $4 billion. (The entire income from the recent Ford Foundation gift for faculty salaries comes to only $10 million a year and is spread out over 615 colleges—only a drop, though a welcome one, in the bucket.)

3. *Residential or non-residential.* If we transform our college system into a predominantly non-residential one, we can get by during the next fifteen or twenty years with an additional $10 to $15 billion or so for buildings and equipment. If, however, we try to stick to our present, predominantly residential, system with its sleeping, eating, and recreational facilities, we may have to spend $40 to $45 billion during the same period. The astronomical quality of these figures takes on a semblance of reality when you consider that facilities for 5 million additional students represent twice as much as all the college plants that have been built in America since Harvard was founded in 1636.

It is fashionable in academic circles to speak rather slightingly of "bricks and mortar" and yet to extol the unique virtues of the residential college. This is inconsistent—dangerously so. If we as a nation want to maintain the residential college we will have to give high priority to bricks and mortar, we may even have to subordinate other needs (such as adequate faculty salaries) to the voracious demands for money for buildings and facilities. This may well be the right decision. The original need for the residential college in a sparsely settled, agricultural country has of course disappeared now that two thirds of our people live in or around metropolitan areas; but the residential college may indeed offer unique advantages and values. Still, we ought to realize that we face a major decision whether we can really afford to retain the predominantly residential character of our colleges; we may even have to decide between preserving residential education and accepting government control in order to obtain the financial support the residential system requires.

4. *The family budget of higher learning.* The final problem is the biggest and cloudiest of all: the cost of higher education to the American family.

College presidents are fond of pointing out that the cost of attending college has gone up less than almost any other major item in the family budget. Statistically this is correct, but it may be irrelevant.

What was a minor cost for the wealthy to whom the colleges looked for their students a generation ago, is today a very large sum to the middle-class family, and an unbearable burden for the 50 per cent of families whose income is below the national average.

It is not uncommon today for a middle-class family to have three children in college at the same time. This means that the bill will run from $4500 to $6000 a year, an all but unbearable charge for the family with an $8000 to $10,000 income. Yet such a family (a bureau chief of a government agency would be in this bracket) would not be considered deserving of scholarship aid by most college administrators who still measure scholarship need by annual family income rather than by the burden of educational costs on the family.

QUESTIONS THAT BREED QUESTIONS

It is the primary purpose of this chapter to raise questions rather than to give answers. But some answers to this financial dilemma have been proposed by educators. Let's look for a moment at two of the most common proposals.

First: there are those who believe that the problem of financing higher education can be solved by more undergraduate scholarships.

It is becoming obvious that new scholarships have to be accompanied by cost-of-education grants to the college; that is, payments to cover the cost of educating a student over and above the amount charged for tuition. The recent scholarship plans of Sears Roebuck, of General Motors, and of the National Merit Scholarship Corporation all have taken this into account. But no amount of scholarship money can possibly bridge the gap, except in a few selective cases, between the costs of going to college and the means available to the average family. Might it not therefore be better to use available new funds to set up graduate scholarships?

Our real problem is not to get more youngsters into the colleges; it is not even to get more able youngsters there. The real problem of enrollment is to get more able undergraduates into graduate and professional schools, and to get more able graduates to go into teaching.

Second: there are many who think that the character of American education can be maintained only through support of the small private college.

The aim of current campaigns to maintain an un-regimented and mixed system of higher education in this country is of course sound. But indiscriminate support of the small, private school—for no other reason than that it is small and private—is by no means the whole answer. Of the 1800 institutions of higher learning in this country two thirds are so small—fewer than 500 students or so— as to be marginal both educationally and financially. Yet no two of these marginal schools are alike.

Some of them have capacity both intellectually and physically for tremendous growth. A good example is North Park College in Chicago, which is affiliated with one of the smallest Protestant denominations, the Mission Covenant Church with 500 congregations and 54,000 communicants. North Park started out as a junior college. Two years ago it converted into a four-year college. Now it is engaged in raising its size from 500 to 1300 students. It has had all along many of the basic facilities—auditorium, library, chapel—needed for a 1300-student four-year college; it just had not utilized them to the full. And while it still needs $4 million in building funds, the affiliated congregations—precisely because they are small and this is their one and only school—have already pledged well over $2 million.

But a great many small colleges can survive only if they team up with other and stronger institutions. In North Carolina, for instance, three Presbyterian-supported junior colleges—total enrollment 500—are being replaced by one four-year school at Laurinburg with an enrollment of 1200.

Some of these marginal colleges might join with the giant universities in co-operative development plans. We certainly do not want institutions with 70,000 or more students under one roof—if only because they subordinate education to administration, and excellence, whether of student or teacher, to procedures. Yet the ten or twenty largest institutions in the country may reach such size within a decade. If instead of growing themselves these giants were to help some smaller affiliated institutions in their area to grow, everybody might gain. The small college might be supplied with administrative and financial guidance and with the attraction of membership in a big-university faculty, while the institutional dropsy and paralysis of the giant would be offset by the independence of the affiliate.

WILL THE COLLEGES BLOW THEIR TOPS?

There are a good many—too many—small private colleges which have not enough to offer, cannot grow, and will not survive, if only because they will not be able to attract new faculty in an era of teacher shortage. Yet it is precisely these that are likely to get the largest share of our scarce financial resources if we concentrate on supporting indiscriminately the small, private schools— simply because they already are in desperate financial straits.

MONEY CHASING

Lack of planning is the greatest weakness of today's approach to the financial crisis of higher education. There are notable exceptions both in large universities and small colleges. But far too many institutions still chase money for individual projects—or just chase money. Far too many base their fund-raising on appeals for the maintenance of the status quo.

Each individual institution needs a plan based on thorough consideration of its educational aims and teaching methods. Too many colleges, for instance, base their building plans on the dubious compromise of the "not-so-very-large" class of forty to fifty students. Yet every experienced teacher knows that this is far too large a group for class discussion or individual work, yet is no better for a lecture course than a group of a hundred. Growth goals, educational aims, curriculum, faculty needs, research plans, facilities planning, architecture, and money need to be pulled together into one integrated program.

Equally important is the choice each college must make between residential and non-residential growth. An increasing number of families will be able to afford unaided only non-residential colleges. Their children will have to save money by living at home and by working part-time to help pay for their tuition.

So unless we develop a greater number of universities that are a combination of residential and non-residential, it is conceivable that American higher education may eventually become entirely non-residential. Some of the large institutions in or near metropolitan centers—Columbia, for instance, and Harvard—have long admitted day students without losing their character as residential institutions.

But there is still another possibility that big universities might well consider. They might "contract out" students in their freshman and sophomore years either to new, non-residential institutions which are set up as part of the university or to existing but presently marginal, small schools. These students might then be admitted to residence at the parent university for their junior and senior years. Or the reverse might be feasible—to have freshmen and sophomores in residence, and juniors and seniors living at home. (Oxford has long used a somewhat similar scheme.)

Finally, colleges need to plan regionally as well as individually. Look for example at what is happening now in Illinois. The University of Chicago and Northwestern, both in the Chicago area, can still increase enrollment without straining their facilities, while the University of Illinois, with its tax subsidy for every in-state student, is bursting its bounds. The University of Illinois is about to build an expensive new campus in Chicago. Would it not be better, let alone cheaper, to adopt the suggestion made by President David Dodds Henry of the University of Illinois, to offer an in-state student the amount he would cost the state if he went to Illinois and let him spend the money to pay tuition at Chicago or Northwestern if he so desires? It would save the state the expense of building a new campus, at least for a few years.

The major conclusion from this outline of the financial crisis of higher education still has to be stated: No matter how good our planning, the financial needs of higher education over the next two decades cannot be met with the resources now available or in sight—including student fees, gifts from individuals, corporations, and foundations, and state or city taxes.

The problem is not one of finding new donors to take the place of the individual rich man of fifty years ago. Indeed private giving to higher education is far higher already than it has ever been. The problem is not primarily one of meeting the costs of inflation. The real problem is that the educational explosion has already blown the inherited financial foundation of American higher education sky-high. We shall have to build an entirely new one—and build it fast.

Today the total annual expenditure of higher education, including capital investment, is probably around $5 billion. Twenty years hence it may exceed $25 billion. At the same time the annual expenditure of grade and secondary schools will also rise from about $10 billion today (for all schools, public, private, and parochial) to $20 or $25 billion.

The total annual cost of education to the American people will therefore rise from some $15 billion today to $50 billion by 1975—with higher education increasing its share from one third to one half of the total budget.

Today about four cents out of every dollar of national income is spent for education. Even if we assume a doubling of national income, we will have to spend seven to eight cents out of every dollar on education twenty years hence.

FUNDS TO BE TAPPED

This means that we cannot dismiss the possibility that federal money will have to become the financial foundation of higher education in America. Yet most of us would regret this solution for reasons that are perfectly sound. Nothing would be less desirable than government control of American higher education—for government finance has meant government control in every other country. Serious thought therefore must be given to how the principles of our higher education can be preserved, despite dependence on government support. We must consider what safeguards would be needed, what new agencies might be created to administer the government grants, and what form government support might take to do the most good and the least harm. If we fail to do this we run the risk of finding ourselves—suddenly and in financial panic—rushing into the worst kind of Ministry of Education—something on the French or Italian model perhaps, uncontrolled and uncontrollable, rigid, pedantic, timid, and yet all-powerful.

But at the same time we also need to work on the much more challenging but also much more difficult job: to find a new, truly private, and yet adequate financial foundation for an American system of *general* higher education.

We are, perhaps, overlooking some of the most fruitful sources of a solution to the problem, sources much more agreeable to us than those which threaten government control. The way in which we have attacked another crisis of American growth—medical and hospital care—may point a direction for coping with the educational explosion. Thirty years ago a compulsory government health plan appeared to be the only way to provide adequate medical and hospital care to the American people. Yet today these services are being handled pretty well through voluntary community organizations and insurance. To be sure, we shall in all probability need some government support— both in money and organization—to take care of a small, marginal part of the problem. But we already cover 65 per cent of the risks for 65 per cent of the population, and we are rapidly developing the means—such as major medical cost insurance—to cover 90 per cent of the risks for some 80 per cent of the population.

Similarly, in every other country the research necessary for an expanding economy is primarily provided by government—or is not provided at all. But here we have during the last twenty-five years increased research expenditures from one tenth of one per cent to one per cent of national income largely through the private efforts of universities and businesses.

This suggests that government need not be the main source of support for higher education. Maybe the family can do the job without being overwhelmed by the cost of college. Take for example the family with three children. The cost of giving these children a college education will be around $36,000, of which the family will be expected to pay $18,000 to $20,000. If this sum is considered a charge against the family income during the years the children actually attend college, it is a heavy burden for all but the very well-to-do. But if this college cost is considered a charge against family income during the entire earning life of the parent—that is against the $160,000 to $360,000 which a middle-class or even a working-class father now earns during his lifetime—the charge is less of a burden than the cost of rent, of clothing, or of food, and no more than the expenditure for recreation.

We already have some applications of this idea in a few union contracts providing for scholarships for the children of employees. Industry might well experiment further with such plans—particularly for white-collar employees—as a promising approach to both employee benefits and to financing education.

Or take the case of the college graduate himself. His education has cost $6000 to $12,000, paid partly by him and partly by the school. As a result of this investment, however, his earning power has been increased by 50 per cent —or by at least $100,000 over his earning life. Is it totally unrealistic to expect of him that he split this increase nine to one with the school—that is, return, over a period of forty years, $10,000 to higher education?

It is the fashion today to stress the tremendous dangers to educational values this educational explosion is creating, and the obstacles it will throw up against the superior education of the exceptional individual. Certainly these dangers are real. But in our justified concern with them, we had better not overlook the audacity of the very idea of higher education as *general* education—its challenge and opportunity, the achievement that made it possible even to entertain it, and the national commitment to the value of education which it implies.

Perhaps we are also too frightened today by the financial and economic problems. We should not forget that they are the result of a noble aspiration: to make higher education in America a classless education. We are still trying to solve the financial problems by finding new class sources of income, especially in the big business corporations. It is proper that business enterprise, our new center of productive wealth and financial power, should support education; business as an employer is a major beneficiary of higher education and could not exist, let alone prosper, without it. But even in the short run, business alone could not provide the financial blood transfusions needed to keep higher education alive. In the long run, reliance on any one source is a mistake if what we honestly strive for is a classless higher education. For this there can be only one foundation: support by all the people.

‹‹‹‹‹‹‹‹‹‹‹‹‹‹‹‹‹‹‹‹‹‹‹‹‹›››››››››››››››››››››

CHAPTER FIVE

America Becomes a "Have-Not" Nation

‹‹‹‹‹‹‹‹‹‹‹‹‹‹‹‹‹‹‹‹‹‹‹‹‹›››››››››››››››››››››

FOR THE LAST ten years, our ventures into international economics have been the most imaginative, the most novel, and the most effective part of America's foreign policy. Now, however, they are becoming stale, obsolescent, and ineffective. The Soviet countries, by a deft shift in cold war strategy, are threatening to take the economic initiative away from us all around the world—leaving us in the sterile role of imitator and defender. Clearly it is time for a change.

Fortunately the opportunity for a change is now opening up before us. In the months just ahead, we shall have a unique chance to start on a radically new foreign economic policy—a policy which not only will satisfy the hopes of the free world but also will fit the needs and ideals of the American people. Indeed, the Suez crisis and its impact demand such a new international economic policy for the United States.

Our old policy was, of course, focused on the postwar emergency. It worked splendidly during the period when relief, repair, and rebuilding were the urgent needs. But this postwar job was finished several years ago—and since our program was originally designed for temporary emergencies, it has been continued on a patchwork basis from year to year to help meet various diplomatic and military crises as they came up. Neither Democratic nor Republican Administrations have yet taken time to work out a permanent policy *specifically designed to serve our own self-interest.*

Indeed, we have not had an *American* economic policy at all; we have had a foreign-aid program. Its unprecedented generosity fired the imagination of our own people. Abroad it rekindled hope, courage, and faith in the future, in a way far more important than the immediate economic impact of our help.

But the very fact that it was a program of foreign aid made Congress perpetually suspicious, and built up a growing opposition to "giveaways" throughout the country. Moreover, once the first emergency was past, this emphasis on aid was bound to breed dissatisfaction and suspicion abroad. The friends we helped were dissatisfied because nobody likes to be cast in the role of a perennial beggar. They were suspicious because they were sure there must be some hidden motive behind such generosity—that the helping hand must be the fist of American imperialism in disguise.

This uneasiness—both in Congress and abroad—was well founded. A foreign policy that is purely selfish is indeed a mean policy, and will come to a mean end. But a policy entirely divorced from national self-interest is equally unsound and impermanent.

There was another flaw in the old policy. It was based on an assumption of extreme economic isolation. The Marshall Plan and Point Four program both assumed—consciously or subconsciously—that the United States is economically independent of the outside world, while the outside world is extremely dependent on the United States. This was well expressed in the slogan of a few years back: "When the United States sneezes, Europe catches pneumonia." Even today most people in this country take it for granted that, economically, America can go it alone—indeed, that America would be better off if there were no outside world with its clamor for American handouts.

This economic isolationism is, however, no less dangerous in today's world than political or military isolationism would be. Worse, it is a complete perversion of reality. In fact the outside world is daily becoming less dependent upon America; this is the meaning of the setbacks our international economic policy experienced during 1955 and 1956 in Egypt, Indonesia, and Latin America. Moreover, the United States is daily becoming more dependent upon the outside world—in particular, upon the raw-material producing countries.

It can be said quite bluntly that international economic relations are the Achilles' heel of the American economy. Our ability to solve the tremendous problems of our dependence on foreigners will very largely determine the

rate of expansion of our economy during the next generation. For the painful truth is that our basic long-range
position in the international economy is not one of
strength, but one of great potential weakness.

The overriding need of the American economy will be to
find a supply of raw materials to keep our industrial machine going. And a rapidly increasing amount of these raw
materials will have to come from abroad.

Our own cupboard—once bountifully stuffed with raw
materials—already has been emptied much more than
most of us realize. The Mesabi iron range, once the world's
greatest source of ore, is almost gone; and we are shipping
in ore to feed our steel mills from Canada, South America,
and Africa. Crude oil, which we used to export in floods,
now has to be imported in increasing amounts. Other raw
materials which are indispensable for our defense and our
daily living—bauxite for aluminum, manganese, nickel,
wood pulp, chrome, and a dozen others—all come largely
from outside our borders. Within fifteen or twenty years,
we may well be the major "have-not" country in the world.

To be sure, we still supply all of our own needs in food
and clothing, and most of our needs for shelter. It is also
true that most other industrial nations will have to import
an even larger share of their raw-material supplies than we
do. But out per-capita import needs will be as large as those
of any other country; and our total volume of imports probably will be as big as that of several of the great industrial
countries of Western Europe lumped together. Today we
have only about 10 per cent of the earth's population, but

we are using up about 50 per cent of the entire world output of raw materials. Obviously our standard of living—
and especially our rate of growth—will become increasingly dependent on our ability to get the raw materials we
need.

This of course is not a new conclusion. It was reached by
the Paley Commission appointed by President Truman in
1951. But the Paley Commission seriously underrated both
the speed of American economic expansion and the rate at
which our demand for raw materials would grow. For instance, it expected American power needs to double within
the next twenty-five years; but the Federal Power Commission—a rather conservative body, judging by its past pre-
dictions—now expects our use of power by 1980 to be
four times our present consumption. Furthermore, developments of the last five years have shown that raw-material
needs increase a great deal faster than production and consumption. In fact they might be said—though the statistical
evidence is not altogether conclusive—to increase twice
as fast.

A SET OF SPECIFICATIONS

Even more important is the fact that the Paley Commission concerned itself exclusively with United States
requirements. It assumed that the rest of the world would
remain unchanged. But raw-material demands are increasing even faster outside the United States—in the rapidly
expanding industries of Western Europe, in the countries
behind the Iron Curtain, and, above all, in the rapidly

75

industrializing nations of Latin America, Australia, Asia, and Africa. In the absence of a world-wide catastrophe, we must assume that the demand for industrial raw materials outside of the United States will continue to grow faster than here, and that twenty years from now the United States will find itself in tough competition for all such imports.

How large our imports needs will be in ten or twenty years cannot be estimated with any accuracy. But it is reasonable to guess that, in order to double our national income within the next fifteen to twenty years—the assumption on which most economists base their forecasts and most business companies their capital investments—we will have to import the equivalent of at least a quarter of our total industrial production. We will have to pay for these imports with equivalent exports—which would mean increasing our imports and exports four times over their present level.

This leads to four major conclusions about the basic aims of a new American economic policy.

First of all, it will have to be a policy that will make it possible for us to *increase exports* fast enough to pay our international bills. We still assume that our exports are only limited by the ability of foreign countries to obtain dollars. It would be safer to base our policy on the assumption that, within a decade, the dollar shortage of yesterday may have disappeared, and that our main problem will be how to earn enough foreign exchange to pay for our imports. The first goal of our new policy, therefore, must be to make the United States capable of selling in a competitive world market, and to make it possible for our potential customers to buy our goods in large volume.

The second aim must be an *expansion of raw-material production throughout the world.* Productive capacity for industrial raw materials, adequate to the world needs of tomorrow, simply does not now exist—even if the needs of the rapidly industrializing countries of the Soviet orbit are completely (and short-sightedly) left out of the calculation.

We cannot expect—as did the Paley Report by implication—that this country can obtain a very much larger share of the world's supply of industrial raw materials at the expense of our friends and allies in the Free World. This would not only be politically undesirable, since it would inevitably destroy our foreign alliances and would produce the "cannibalistic conflict of the Imperialists" on which Soviet policy banks. It simply is not possible. In the event of a real shortage of raw materials, the supplier countries are bound to use whatever they produce for their own growing industries, rather than to stunt their own growth for the sake of the American economy.

The third goal for a permanent international economic policy must be *to harmonize our own self-interest with the aspirations and interests of the peoples of the Free World.* Increasingly we will be dependent on their willingness to be closely integrated with the American economy. This co-operation cannot be forced, and it cannot be bought.

It has to be earned through a policy that clearly and imaginatively merges the openly avowed self-interest of America and the national self-interest of our partners.

Finally such a policy must *strengthen the Free World socially and politically*—that is, it must symbolize its beliefs and values, and must express the reality of responsible American leadership.

There is one—and only one—policy that will answer all these requirements. That is for America to take the lead in promoting the rapid economic growth—and especially the rapid industrial growth—of the raw-material producing countries.

The simplest way to illustrate this is to contrast India and Switzerland. India—with almost 400 million inhabitants and with a fair supply of dollar exchange supplied primarily by American aid—buys less from the United States and sells less to the United States than does Switzerland. Yet Switzerland has less than 5 million people and is completely independent of American aid. In other words, it is industrial production and economic well-being that create the need for imports, the purchasing power to buy them, and the capacity to produce exports to pay for them. If India could double her miserably low standard of living, both her industrial imports and her raw-material exports might well increase tenfold. But India can double her standard of living only by rapid industrialization.

What is true of India is true of all the other pre-industrial countries, which are the main sources of our raw-materials.

The rapid industrialization of the countries that produce raw materials is, therefore, the best investment the United States can make in its own economic future. It is, moreover, the foremost ambition of these countries themselves. And it is a job which the United States—both because we were ourselves a raw-material producing country only a few short decades ago and because we are the leading industrial society today—should be pre-eminently fitted to make our own.

RECIPE FOR GROWTH

We have learned a good deal about economic growth these last few years—so much that we can now say what it requires.

We do not, indeed, yet have anything that could be called an adequate theory of economic growth; but at least we know that the old assumptions once accepted by both economists and businessmen were all wrong.

The essential thing is not that an economy is "backward" or "underdeveloped," as even President Truman still assumed when he announced the Point Four program. The real point is that an economy has to have a potential of growth. (The sooner we rid our language of such terms as "backward" and "underdeveloped," the more successful our policy will be. In addition to being misleading, they are condescending to the point of insult.) Any sound policy must aim at the *economic self-development of "growth" countries.*

This is important not only because it makes possible a

79

positive approach, instead of the cavity-filling and trouble-shooting approach of a program of aid to underdeveloped areas. Above all it makes possible systematic planning with clear priorities—the method we have learned to use with conspicuous success in large-scale business. In fact, some of the disciplines developed in the last few years for the analysis of business decisions—such as, for instance, Operations Research and Synthesis—seem singularly applicable in diagnosing opportunities of a growth economy.

We also know that economic development is not a slow, continuous process, but one of leap-frogging. It does not proceed step-by-step, but in break-throughs. And it is not exclusively—maybe not even primarily—an economic process; it also involves a deep cultural and social change —a change in values, habits, knowledge, attitudes, ways of life, social ideals, and aspirations.

Most important of all, we have learned what a country needs to make these changes—with the minimum of social, political, and cultural upheaval. There are three main requirements:

1. *A demand for investment capital* must be created. Traditional economic theory assumed that the supply of investment capital determined whether a country would grow industrially, and how fast. But we have now found that a pre-industrial country usually has more capital than investment opportunities. Capital by itself is sterile; and its lack, while painful, is rarely an absolute bar to growth. But opportunities for investment—that is, for risk-taking, productive enterprise—are economic lifeblood.

2. *"Multiplier industries"* must be created. These are the industries that will set off economic chain reactions, thus producing industrial skill, activity, and enterprise out of all proportion to their own size. We even know that there are four categories of such multiplier industries and that for maximum growth a country needs a balanced diet of all four.

There are "spectaculars," such as our Western railroads in the second half of last century, or the TVA in the thirties. In themselves, these are almost always unprofitable, indeed wasteful; but they have a major impact because they so visibly symbolize the new age with its new possibilities of conquering nature, its values, and its new horizons.

There are community services—transportation facilities and power supply above all—which create an integrated economy out of fragmented and isolated districts.

There are service industries to make effective the two kinds of demand needed to move forward the wheels of an industrial economy: (a) a distribution system to create consumer demand, and (b) a credit system to create effective investment demand. For example, the revolutionary impact of a few Sears Roebuck stores on the economic development of Mexico, Brazil, and Colombia cannot be exaggerated. By United States standards their total sales volume is almost negligible. Yet these stores have put into business a host of new, home-owned and home-managed manufacturing industries. They have opened new careers and created new standards of industrial technology and industrial management. They have pushed up productivity

—and with it wages and purchasing power. Finally they are forcing the entire retail system where they operate to change from selling at high profit and in low volume, to low-profit, high-volume merchandising for a homogeneous mass market.

And—the fourth multiplier category—at different times and places, different manufacturing industries have a multiplier effect. In Monterey, Mexico—one of the fastest growing and most modern industrial areas in this hemisphere—a brewery apparently served as the first multiplier through its demands for bottles, bottle caps, trucks, and so on. In our own Southeast, tiremaking and automobile assembly seem to have had this effect of multiplying economic growth—an effect which was not produced at an earlier stage either by the textile industry or by the huge but economically inert steel mills of Birmingham, Alabama.

3. The most important requirement of rapid industrial growth is *people*. People trained to be entrepreneurs, managers, marketers, investment and commercial bankers, engineers, geologists, and technicians of many varieties. People ready to welcome the challenge of economic change and the opportunities in it. People, above all, who are dedicated to the economic development of their country, and to high standards of honesty, competence, knowledge, and performance. What is needed beyond all else is leadership and example; and those only the right kind of people can provide.

Any policy that tries to supply money or facilities without at the same time providing people in quantity and in quality must inevitably fail. It may even do harm. And the people must emerge fast; the entire pre-industrial world is in a ferment—is eagerly, almost explosively, looking to economic progress as its road to salvation. If American international economic policy does not succeed in developing the trained and dedicated people whom the growth countries need, they will look elsewhere for the answers and for the leadership.

ARE WE "IMPERIALIST"?

To a considerable extent, this is a matter of providing skills—in accounting, in industrial engineering, in metallurgy, or in management. But skills are not enough; they are not even the main thing. For the real challenge is to capture the vision and the energies of the young trained people in each country—the young people who are eager to lead and to serve, who want to do something great with their lives, and who aspire to no mean end. These men will have to learn skills, of course; for without skills dedication and zeal are futile. But they will not be satisfied with skills alone. Nor should they be. (The Communists learned this long ago; that is why they specialize in zeal.)

The extent to which industrial growth satisfies these people will decide how fast and how successfully a country grows, and also whether this growth will lead it into full membership in the Free World or toward the totalitarian abyss.

All growth countries require two things to develop the

people they need. They require something that is intellectually and aesthetically satisfying: an organized body of
knowledge—that is, a discipline of entrepreneurship and
management. And they require social and moral principles
of business conduct which a good man can respect and
on which he can build self-respect.

The main grievance which the pre-industrial world has
against the Europeans is that they have failed, during their
century of economic leadership, to produce native leaders
who could guide the modern industrial development of
their own countries. This is, at bottom, what an Indonesian
means when he talks about "Western economic imperialism." It is a legitimate grievance. For people are the only
enduring resource of a society.

If our new international economic policy fails to stim-
ulate the self-development of the kind of people needed in
the growth countries, it cannot succeed. It will then be regarded—no matter how noble and unselfish our intentions,
or how open our pocketbook—as just another device of the
"colonialist" and "exploiter." But if the development of
trained and dedicated people is made a clear priority, then
our new policy may well succeed in building a co-operative
and productive world economy—the kind of economy on
which our own prosperity (if not survival) increasingly
depends.

Fortunately this is the one part of the job where we are
somewhat ahead. Marshall Plan and Point Four—though
almost by accident in the beginning—put heavy emphasis
on the development of people. We called it "technical

assistance" and we talked about "know-how." Yet both the foreign businessmen who came here as members of productivity teams, and the American businessmen who have been going abroad on productivity missions, learned that it is not techniques and gadgets that really matter. What does matter is intellectual discipline and an ethical attitude toward the job to be done. They learned fast that the real secret of American economic strength is respect for human beings as the basic resource—rather than a concept of labor as a cost—and the use of people as a social, intellectual, moral, and spiritual resource, rather than as a purely economic one.

As a result every country—even those truly underdeveloped countries, such as France, which are frozen in an antiquated form of European capitalism—has a fairly large number of people in business and industry who are eager, who are reaching out, who are ready to assume leadership. They are the real capital resource of the Free World; and each one is worth a regiment. This country today has hundreds, if not several thousands, of businessmen and managers who are graduates of Marshall Plan and Point Four work. There are, in every country—from India to Peru—men in national industry who have developed for themselves the knowledge, the skills, the integrity, and the dedication needed: men who can easily hold their own against our best. And there is a tremendous desire to learn and to develop on the part of business managers throughout the free world. When the Chileans, for instance, organized in the fall of 1956 the first International

Management Congress in South America they had to turn away for lack of space more than four hundred applicants. Yet when they first planned the Congress everybody thought their attendance goal of five hundred to be so ambitious as to be utopian. But these resources of dedication and desire are no more than the raw material. To built a "product" from them, a purposeful and imaginative American economic policy is needed.

WHAT IT WILL TAKE

Such a policy will first require a change in our attitude toward the international economy. Our participation in the industrial development of the growth countries would have to be regarded as an investment in our own economic future, rather than as aid to foreigners.

It will require a long-range commitment—for ten or twenty years—not necessarily to any specific amount of money, but to the principles of the program. It will also require, however, a fair amount of money—to finance spectaculars such as large dams; to provide services such as transportation, power, and irrigation projects; and to insure American investors against currency and expropriation risks. We must also recognize that rapidly industrializing countries occasionally suffer sudden economic upsets, such as the ones that trouble Turkey and Brazil today (and troubled the United States in 1837, 1873, and 1894.) Quick short-term financial help, though in fairly small amounts, is sometimes needed to prevent such an upset stomach from turning into a wasting disease.

We shall also have to contribute American help to diagnose growth opportunities and plan economic development. We shall have to contribute knowledge, advice, technical assistance, and educational facilities. And finally we shall have to contribute people of our own.

This is to a considerable degree a job for the federal government. The government will have to raise whatever money is needed, whether in the form of loans or of grants. It will have to negotiate the agreements with foreign countries under which the policy operates. (To be effective, this has to be a truly co-operative policy, carried out in partnership with the growth countries, and separate from any program of short-range emergency relief or military alliance.)

The other industrially developed countries of the Free World—Western Europe, Japan, and Australia—should be encouraged to join in a policy that is as much in the interest of their survival as it is in ours. And as soon as growth countries emerge industrially, they should become associated as leaders with the international development program. This would make the policy truly co-operative, rather than purely American. Moreover, the experience gained and the people available in such recent growth areas as Turkey, Puerto Rico, São Paulo, or Bombay are particularly useful and should be tapped.

The government also will have to work out the conditions under which an American business investing abroad might become eligible for re-insurance against the risks of expropriation and currency devaluation. (Criteria might be, for instance: Is the investment in a growth country? Is it in an industry which is relatively new to the country and which is still, technologically or in its capital requirements, beyond the reach of local businessmen? Does it save the country several times the foreign exchange for imports that is required to service the capital investment? Is it a multiplier industry? Does it have an organized program for training local people within a reasonable period for managerial and technical positions?) And of course the government would also have to serve as the co-ordinator for the entire program—indeed the International Co-operation Administration would have to be made a permanent government agency.

But this is not a job government could, or should, do alone. A major part of it will have to be done by the American companies operating abroad. Far too many of them still reserve their managerial and technical jobs for Americans and Europeans—though in Latin America the oil companies, the Grace interests, and Sears are shining exceptions. Far too many also follow managerial practices in their foreign subsidiaries they would never tolerate at home.

Finally this is a job for all American business and managers (and in large measure for American labor leaders). It is a job they will find hard. The systematic knowledge of entrepreneurship and management, which they will have to exemplify and to teach, is barely in its beginning in this country, and is yet to be acquired even in its rudiments by most of our businessmen. And the social and moral principles, which they will have to practice and to convey are still preachments for many of them.

It is a job that will require time, effort, and humility. Yet, performance of this job will decide whether the manager is worthy of the leadership role our business society has entrusted to him. It may also decide whether this business society of ours can survive.

Above all, a responsible policy, adequate to our own needs and focused on the rapid self-development of the growth countries, will require imaginative, bold leadership at the very top. In the Point Four program—and in the parallel Technical Assistance program of the United Nations—we have a foundation of experience, achievement, and dedication. In President Eisenhower's current proposal to put "foreign aid" on a long-term basis we have made the first step toward an effective policy. Prominent groups, such as the Committee for Economic Development, are demanding sharp increases in foreign aid, especially to Latin America, the Near East and Asia. But much of this is still conceived as an answer to Communist pressure rather than as a basic long-range American need and self-interest.

Ten years ago, with a few quiet words spoken on a summer afternoon, George Catlett Marshall—appealing to the heads and hearts of his countrymen rather than to their pocketbooks—created a new vision for America and changed the fate of Western Europe. The danger today may be even greater. But so is the opportunity.

❮❮❮❮❮❮❮❮❮❮❮❮❮❮❮❮❮❮❮❮❮❮❮❮❮❮❯❯❯❯❯❯❯❯❯❯❯❯❯❯❯❯❯❯❯❯❯

CHAPTER SIX

Coming Issues
in American Politics

❮❮❮❮❮❮❮❮❮❮❮❮❮❮❮❮❮❮❮❮❮❮❮❮❮❮❯❯❯❯❯❯❯❯❯❯❯❯❯❯❯❯❯❯❯❯❯

WE HAVE REACHED a major watershed in American politics. Behind us are sixty years of great issues and constant change—the sixty years from Mark Hanna to Walter Reuther, from Booker T. Washington to the Supreme Court decision outlawing racial segregation in the schools, from Bryan's "Cross of Gold" speech to today's slogan of "People's Capitalism," from the electric streetcar to the hydrogen bomb. During these sixty years the United States has transmuted itself from an agrarian into an industrial society and from isolation into leadership as a world power.

The issues and slogans of these sixty years were still echoed, all but automatically, in last Fall's election campaign, seemed indeed at times to dominate it. But rarely in our history has campaign oratory fallen on deafer ears, sounded flatter, or meant less. For if the four years of the first Eisenhower Administration meant anything, they meant that the New Deal, in which all these issues of the past sixty years had culminated, finally passed into history, codified, consolidated, and accepted.

We have still to come to grips with the issues that are likely to dominate the decades ahead. One would have to go back to Franklin D. Roosevelt's First Hundred Days in 1933 to find anything comparable to the steady stream of proposals on major policy and requests for major legislation—on transportation, inflation, water use, medical care, education, tariff policy and so on—that President Eisenhower poured out in the early months of 1956. Every one of these proposals would have seemed radical, if not revolutionary, a few years ago. That only one of these proposals—the Highway Bill—became law, is therefore perhaps not too remarkable. But that none of them became a great issue, capable of arousing emotions, of organizing political alignments, or of being seriously debated in a campaign, indicates that we as a nation are still resting from the work of the past and not ready yet to tackle the jobs of tomorrow. Or rather we still—and that clearly goes for both parties—believe that these are the "jobs of tomorrow."

But "tomorrow," as the preceding chapters of this book have tried to show, is largely already accomplished fact. And tomorrow's issues in American politics can therefore already be identified, defined, and described by an analysis of the future that has already happened.

THE NEW MIGRATION

One starting point of this analysis, and one central fact, is, of course, the growth of our population and the changes in its structure. Equally important is its shift in geographic distribution. Twenty years ago, when it was commonly believed that America's population had ceased to grow, it was also widely held that our people had lost their traditional mobility. "The days of the frontier are forever gone," and so on. The past ten or fifteen years have proved this false. The largest migration in our history began during World War II; and it has continued ever since with undiminished momentum.

This is a migration both of people and of industry. Three areas in particular have grown as fast as any on this continent ever did in the past: the Far West, the Southwest, and—just north of the border but intimately linked with the United States—Southern Ontario. To be sure, the spectacular growth of California—from fifth in size of population in 1940 to second in 1950—shows signs of slowing down. But even so, California will be the most populous state by 1965, if not by 1960. And Texas, New Mexico, Nevada, Oregon, and Florida are now growing at boom speed. Just across the border, Southern Ontario since the end of the war has become one of the major industrial areas of the world; and the opening of the St. Lawrence Seaway should bring another tremendous expansion to Canada's industrial center.

The new migration is an urban one. California is already one of the most highly urbanized states in the Union; and Southern Ontario is hardly less urban, despite all attempts by the Canadian government to direct into farming the "New Canadians" from Europe. Internal migration from the farm to the city is also changing the character of the Old South. Fifteen years ago the states that once formed the Confederacy were predominantly agricultural; only one out of every four people employed held a non-farm job. Today half the Southern population makes its living away from the farm. And, significantly, the Southern Negro seems to have become urbanized even faster than the Southern white.

Already, in other words, the Americans are a *metropolitan* people. Almost two-thirds of us live and work in the 168 areas the Census recognizes as metropolitan. The country can in fact be best envisaged as a galaxy of urban solar systems. And while, within itself, every one of the metropolitan systems tends to decentralize—as people move to the suburbs—the country as a whole tends steadily to centralize. It is the push of people toward the metropolis that causes it to expand into the semi-urban countryside.

The basic issues of domestic policy in the next twenty years will therefore be those of a densely populated industrial country in which the metropolitan area is the basic unit. There will no longer be major regional differences in basic population patterns. Even in Colorado, Utah, and Arizona well over half the population is already metropolitan. Above all, the basic difference between the agrarian South and the industrial or commercial North—which has shaped so much of American history and culture—is bound to become increasingly just a memory.

These population developments by themselves are producing new basic issues of national policy, requiring broad national as well as local or regional resolution.

NEW ISSUE: WATER

The geography textbooks have it that the United States is favored above all nations with natural resources. But there is one natural resource in which the United States, compared to Western Europe, has always been badly supplied. It is a basic one: *water*. Not only is rainfall over large parts of the country deficient, and abundant rainfall limited to small areas in the Northwest and Southeast; but because of geography, geology, or soil structure far too much of the rainfall we get seems to be lost in run-off rather than stored up in the subterranean water table for future use.

During the past fifteen years the signs have multiplied that we are living off our water capital—running the risk of repeating with our water resources the orgy of destruction we indulged in with our soil. Water tables, once depleted, are even more difficult to restore than eroded and depleted soil. Yet we continuously pour new population and new industries into areas of marginal water supply, inviting disasters that we should have experience enough to forestall.

During the next twenty years the need for water will sharply increase, partly because of population growth, but mainly because the new and growing industries typically need water at an ever-increasing rate. A mad scramble for the *allocation* of water resources among metropolitan areas, states, and regions is already going full tilt—between New York and Philadelphia in the East, for example: between California, Oregon, Nevada, Arizona, New Mexico, and Colorado in the West. There will be so many of these fights for a larger share of an inadequate water supply— and they will be so bitter—that federal water allocation is certain to be demanded and heatedly discussed.

The conservation of water will be a more novel—and certainly a more intense—political issue. Twenty years hence, in many parts of the United States, the users of water (especially industrial ones) will have to re-use it and to return it, cleaned and cooled, to the underground water table—an expensive process. State laws or local ordinances on water conservation should therefore be the hottest of political hot potatoes nearly everywhere in the country from now on.

The same has already begun to apply to conservation of all kinds: soil and forests; grazing lands and petroleum; clean, unpolluted air and clean, unpolluted water; scenic beauty and open spaces. All of these will be continuously more desirable, more expensive, and more difficult to secure—and hence they will become even more prominent as political issues for national and local governments alike.

POWER, TRANSPORTATION, AND HOUSING

The population pattern will also push into the foreground our national policies on all three of these basic facilities: power, transportation, and housing.

Our power needs will grow even faster than our water needs. Broadly speaking, technology is now moving from the age of mechanical industry into that of chemicals (where, for instance, atomic energy belongs). Electric power is the basic raw material of most chemical industries; and our present power supply, despite the tremendous building of new stations in the past ten years, is already inadequate. Need will continue to grow faster than supply. Most of the accessible sources of water-generated power have already been used up. From now on we will have to depend increasingly on thermal generation.

Already this has again raised the issue of the large governmental power system like TVA or Bonneville. They can only keep up with demand if they add thermal generating facilities. And whether they do this by building their own generating stations or by going into partnership with private companies, they are bound to arouse antagonism and debate. That much, at least, the Dixon-Yates contract can be said to have proved.

At the same time, however, as atomic power reactors are being developed, the basic technology of thermal power generation is changing. This will raise an even touchier political issue. The Atomic Energy Act of 1954, a major landmark in the relationship of government to private business, decided for the private development of the new resource. It did so, however, not merely by applying to atomic power the traditional and uniquely American principle of close regulation of private industry by public authority. It also for the first time established partnership between public bodies and private industry—and inevitably so, since atomic power cannot be wholly divorced from atomic war material. Even if the 1954 act were a clearer and less ambiguous document than it is, these twin features (regulation and partnership) would by themselves insure that the status of the power industry in relation to government will for years remain a source of contention.

Transportation needs, too, are fast outgrowing their facilities. During the past year we committed ourselves to making our highways adequate to the needs of an industrial continent. The program is certainly a giant step forward. Yet, though the Highway Bill of 1956 is the biggest and most ambitious program of "internal improvements" ever enacted in this country, it almost certainly will prove too little and too late within five years or so. As it stands it will give us, by 1970 or so, the highway system we already need today. And the attempt to shoehorn the program into the existing machinery of federal and state governments is unlikely to work; at the least it must seriously hamper the carrying out of the program within its limits of time and money.

Railroad regulation still assumes a transportation monopoly of the railroads, where the actual conditions of monopoly have long since disappeared. The Grand Canyon mid-air collision last summer showed dramatically how poorly equipped we are to organize tomorrow's air traffic. And there is no co-ordination of policy—even less, of regulating agencies—between rail, highway, and airway transportation. It has been obvious since the mid-thirties that the creation of a unified Department of Transportation at cabinet level would make good sense. Even more necessary —and more controversial—are national programs for building and maintaining a transport system adequate to our population and industry.

Housing will be a major political issue—nationally as well as locally. We are at present building in the new industrial areas some of the worst slums this country has ever seen—in and around Los Angeles, for example, and in the new industrial cities of the South. These new slums are expensive, but the fact that a tarpaper shack costs $14,000 does not make it any less of a shack.

The housing need, moreover, will grow mightily before it lessens. As every suburban home owner knows, we live today off the housing inheritance of our grandparents. Few middle-class families could afford to build the kind of house they are now able to live in, thanks to the lower building costs of thirty years ago. But these houses are rapidly deteriorating. Within the next twenty years most of them will have to be replaced. Together these older houses constitute the bulk of our available, and practically all of our good, housing. But they are rarely to be found, unfortunately, in the areas of maximum population growth. Here we will need large numbers of new houses. These had better be reasonably decent, reasonably cheap, and reasonably well built—and we will want to get them without state or federal entry, except for slum clearance, into the housing business.

PRESSURE ON THE SCHOOLS

Another area of constant concern, at all levels of government, will be education. Today we are at least 75,000 classrooms short of the minimum needs of our children in primary and secondary schools. This means that 1.5 million children cannot be properly educated—half of them are on double or triple sessions; half go to school in temporary barracks, unused garages, or church basements. Of the school buildings now in existence, one fifth are fire traps long past their maximum life span.

We are building 50,000 new classrooms a year, but that is less than we need to take care of the yearly growth in school population. The deficit is not being reduced; it grows by 10 or 20,000 classrooms a year. And in the mid-sixties another huge increase in school population will overtake us. And this is only the need in primary and secondary schools, to which must be added the needs of colleges and universities for additional facilities.

In the light of these needs President Eisenhower's school-building proposals of last year were indeed as inadequate as the harshest critics said they were. Even so, however, both parties in Congress were clearly only too happy to be able to use the segregation issue as a pretext for doing nothing about school construction.

At that they may have been wise. For physical facilities are but one aspect of the great education issue that looms on the American political horizon. They are the one aspect moreover that can be dealt with by paying out money. The others require something a good deal scarcer and more controversial: hard thinking about values, objectives, and policies.

There is first the need for teachers. Earlier in this book this was shown to be central to the problems higher education faces. But we also need teachers—many, many more—on all other levels, from kindergarten through senior high school. Yet, instead of training more teachers, we are training fewer today than we did twenty years ago.

Educational policy and curriculum also promise to become central issues. At present there is little left of the fervent interest in education that characterized the thirties; but now is the very moment when the pressure of numbers on the schools should force them into experiments with new methods, new subjects, and new educational policies. Moreover, the more going to college becomes the normal thing for the young American to do, the more crucial becomes the question of harmonizing academic freedom with education for citizenship—a problem by no means as easy to solve as it appears to either liberal or reactionary.

MEDICAL CARE FOR EVERYONE

During the next two decades we will also have to decide how to make medical and hospital care available to everyone. Already we have begun to tackle this problem through voluntary community co-operation; Blue Cross and Blue Shield are the obvious examples. We have yet to extend this system to the self-employed, the farmers, the very poor, and the aged. Above all, we have to extend it to cover major medical expenses or catastrophic illness expenses—the most serious medical costs for all but the very rich. The abortive proposal of the Eisenhower Administration to re-insure catastrophic illness insurance by co-operatives and private companies—and thus make it available to those who cannot be covered today—was thus a major step in the right direction.

There is also the question of providing for medical education. We do not train even enough doctors today to take care of an expanding population at our present standard. Any extension of medical cost insurance to make adequate medical care more easily available would create a *real* doctor shortage. Yet, medical education is so expensive that it puts medical school expansion beyond the reach of even the few rich universities. A good case can be made out for considering the cost of medical education as a long-term capital investment, which the doctor's higher earning power should enable him to repay over the years. Even such self-financing of medical education, however, might require some form of public re-insurance of the risk; and though the amounts would be fairly small, they are not going to be easy to find.

DECLINE OF THE UNIONS?

Nor are the next twenty years likely to be years of industrial peace. On the contrary, all signs point to labor ferment: the rapid rise of total population without an accompanying rise of working population; the major technological shifts which will change large numbers of jobs from unskilled work to highly skilled; the resulting need for radical change in concepts of seniority and training; and the rapid growth of industry in sparsely unionized areas. Unrest may arise not merely between management and labor but fully as much, perhaps even more, between labor and the public, and within labor itself.

There is today a large area of agreement on the rights and limitations of trade unions throughout the country—far larger than the shrill battle cries of small minorities on either side would lead you to suspect.

But there are four unresolved issues—each a basic one. There is the strike that imperils national welfare. There is the conflict between union security and the right to work. There are the union restrictions of access to a craft. And finally there is the fight over the unionization of employees who are not industrial workers—salaried employees, clerks, engineers, and so on. Since the work population will before long be dominated by white-collar employees, their acceptance or rejection of unionization will determine whether the labor union will continue to be a power in industrial society or become just another pressure group—and a rather insulated and rapidly aging one at that.

DEMAND FOR EQUALITY

We can expect the status of the Negro minority, during the next two decades, to change fairly drastically. Twenty years hence, the rapid industrialization of the South—combined with the continuous emigration of Negroes from the South—should mean that the traditional Southern pattern of rural and small-town segregation, except for a few isolated areas, will be a thing of the past.

Indeed the Supreme Court decision on integration in the schools may, in the long run, prove to have been a rear-guard action—though an important and highly significant one—rather than the break-through. To be sure, half of our Negro population still lives in the South. But the proportion of young Negroes of school age still in the South is already very much less; and even fewer Negro children live in the rural areas where integration will be fought the hardest.

Increasingly therefore, race relations will become problems of the industrial city, and especially of the Northern industrial city. For the future of race relations in this country what happens in Buffalo, Indianapolis, and Flint is already a great deal more important than what happens in Mississippi.

Increasingly, within the next twenty years, we can therefore expect the Negro's fight for equal opportunity and fair treatment to shift from a demand for equal employment opportunities to a demand for equal opportunities for advancement. While this would represent a tremendous achievement—nothing less than the attainment of economic equality for the American Negro—it would also encounter more resistance. Certainly a national policy focused on the steady and courageous pursuit of Negro equality—and based upon a firm insistence on the Negroes' civil and economic rights—will be badly needed during this period.

The economic forces which determine the employment of older workers—that is, over sixty-five—will pull in opposite directions. Wherever industry shifts to Automation, they will be under pressure to get out. This is not only the easiest way to take care of reductions in employment, it will also be more efficient; the old worker will have the greatest difficulty in re-learning and acquiring new skills. But elsewhere, in the absence of Automation, the shortage of labor will tend to force business to employ old people as long as they are able and willing to work. We will see pressure, therefore, toward better provisions and legislation to prevent discrimination against the older worker. Since the older people will continue, though slowly, to grow in numbers and proportion—at least 12 if not 15 per cent of the population will be over sixty-five by 1975—they may well achieve highly organized and powerful pressure. It would certainly be no more than prudent for both management and union leaders to prepare immediately to determine which of the older people are capable of work, how to place them in jobs they can carry, and how to treat them with respect to lay-offs and promotion. In several states, unions are already clamoring for a Fair Employment Practices Act to forbid discrimination in both hiring and retirement on grounds of age.

NEW IDEAS ABOUT MONEY

These are certainly not going to be years of low government spending—even if armaments expenditures, God willing, should become less necessary. There will be no "withering away of the state," whether Republicans or Democrats control the federal and state governments. Yet our notions of fiscal policy are still based largely on the assumption that high expenditure belongs only in an emergency. How, therefore, are we to combine the needs of the government for large revenue with the needs of an expanding economy for investment capital? Perhaps we may even have to give up the oldest principle of business taxation: the legal distinction between interest on fixed capital—which is considered a cost, and thus deductible from business profits—and the income on venture capital, which is profit and taxed. For under the present high corporation tax rates one dollar paid out in interest costs a company only fifty cents, while a dollar dividend to the stockholder actually requires two dollars in profit. The result of this disproportion is an increased dependence on fixed capital, a decreasing supply of venture capital, and a decreasing revenue therefrom—that is, both economic and fiscal decay.

Another unresolved conflict in fiscal policy lies between the realities of modern governmental life, which require planned long-term capital expenditures, and the constitutional requirement that Congress appropriate money on an annual basis. That no one Congress can commit a future Congress is sound doctrine. But much of the expenditure of modern government is meaningless unless it is considered in long-range terms. Actually, by refusing to accept the reality of a capital budget, Congress may well be sacrificing its control over expenditures. But how

105

such problems as these should be resolved, let alone how they can be resolved, we are clearly not going to know for some time to come.

FOOTNOTE ON INFLATION

On one issue of fiscal policy, public opinion rather than government action may make the greatest difference. That is inflation.

Public opinion in economic matters is still deeply influenced by the depression psychology; it sees in unemployment the major threat and in full employment the earthly paradise. As a result, we have created defenses in depth against the last depression. We are committed to immediate government action the moment there is significant unemployment. And we have such a tremendous backlog of public works—not to mention armaments—that we could immediately mobilize the entire economy should the real threat of unemployment appear.

But the next depression is most unlikely to be an unemployment-depression. One of our greatest economists, the late Joseph Schumpeter of Harvard, pointed out in his last paper—read to the American Economic Association in December 1949, only a few days before his death—that it is inflation rather than unemployment that destroys society in the twentieth century. Schumpeter based his pessimistic appraisal of America's chances to survive as a free society on his belief that American public opinion did not understand the danger of inflation, and would not permit adequate safeguards against it.

Six years later, the keenest European student of the American economy, Felix Somary, the Swiss banker, who had correctly predicted every single economic development in this country from the mid-twenties on, echoed the warning. In a talk given at Harvard in June 1956 Somary was even more emphatic about the danger of inflation, yet even more pessimistic regarding America's will to avoid it.

Inflation is more than an impersonal and general danger to society—the breeder of class hatred and the destroyer of the middle class. In an economy where the great mass of people have become long-term creditors (through their insurance and pension holdings), and where as much as half of the employed population is on fixed salaries which do not readily adjust to changes in money values, inflation may cause more individual suffering than even widespread unemployment. This statement—obvious to any German, Frenchman, Italian, or Austrian (not to mention the people behind the Iron Curtain)—is still incomprehensible to most Americans. While we will not, and should not, forget the danger of an unemployment depression, we will have to learn that it is a major duty of government in our economy to safeguard monetary stability. And this requires, above all, a vigilant public opinion.

The first Eisenhower Administration did well by the country, therefore, in its willingness to brake incipient inflation twice, in 1953 and 1956. Yet quite clearly, public opinion neither understood nor supported these moves. And the administration itself did not dare to admit the obvious: that inflation cannot be prevented or stopped without temporary discomfort and unpleasantness. Yet, sooner or later, within the next decade or two the point will certainly be reached when these facts can no longer be hidden, and when the issue of inflation will have to be joined.

Whatever policies we adopt in these basic areas, their total impact on our national life will be enormous—greater even than that of the New Deal. Certainly—and deservedly—we will debate each one of them, will disagree about them, will engage in bitter partisan fights. But it is doubtful whether the answers adequate to our needs can be developed entirely through the give-and-take of political battle. What we should have are fundamental state papers on the economic and social policies of an industrial society —papers comparable, perhaps, to Jefferson's "Notes on the State of Virginia," Hamilton's "Report on Manufacturers," Henry Clay's "American System," or John Wesley Powell's papers on the management of the Western lands. President Truman made a start in this task by appointing commissions on Water Policy and on Raw Material Resources. The Eisenhower Administration tackled the job of high-way modernization. It opened up for discussion government reinsurance against catastrophic illness, a national transportation policy, and federal aid to education. Its fiscal policy has revealed an awareness of the perils of inflation. But these are only beginnings.

REDRAWING THE MAP

The federal government is the proper agency to develop broad policies in most of these areas. But the federal government simply cannot do the detailed job in any one of them. Much of the actual work will have to be done by local governments—municipal, state, regional. In most areas it will have to be done in close co-operation with private industry. It will have to take account of local or regional needs and circumstances, and the administration will have to be local. Yet existing local and state governments are patently unequal to the task.

The national population no longer corresponds to the traditional distinctions between local and state government. A metropolitan people cuts across the boundary lines of cities, counties, and states. And our political scientists increasingly believe that even the most "local" of these issues require a co-ordinated effort that embraces an entire "super-metropolis" such as the Eastern seaboard from Portland, Maine, to Norfolk, Virginia. The truly admirable system of parkways built by New Jersey, for instance, has only added to the traffic problems of New York, Pennsylvania, and Maryland. The best planning New Jersey can do has been largely nullified, in turn, by the lack of co-ordination with neighboring states. Similarly, Westchester County shows that schools can no longer be planned within the historical unit of the school district. One of the few communities in Westchester that planned ahead for tomorrow's school needs was Pleasantville. But the main effect of Pleasantville's foresight has been an influx of people from the surrounding towns, which has quickly rendered Pleasantville's careful plans inadequate.

Local and state governments, our oldest civic institutions, have remained basically unchanged since the Northwest Ordinance of 1787. But somehow we are going to have to invent and develop new ones that cut across existing jurisdictions. Leonard D. White of the University of Chicago has recently shown (in his three books *The Federalists, The Jeffersonians,* and *The Jacksonians*) how important the administrative foundations laid in the early years of the Republic were for the survival and growth of the United States, and how much courage and imagination went into their design. The creative skill required to build the regional institutions needed now will hardly be of a lesser order.

Our geographic ideas also need revision in the matter of atomic dispersal—a subject that has occasioned more confused talk than action. We now know, at last, that the largest theoretically possible bomb is limited both in its area of immediate danger and of total destruction. We know, too, that there is no defense against atomic attack; there is only early warning—and even this is problematical with guided intercontinental missiles. Finally we know— though it is highly secret information—what are the critical products and processes on which our ability to maintain an industrial economy really depends.

We know what we need to know, in other words, to escape paralysis from the first all-out attack. It should be emphasized that dispersal is not defense. It is only a safe-guard against being knocked out in the first round. And it is not something we have actually achieved. In fact we may be more vulnerable today than we were ten years ago. Forty per cent of the American population and 56 per cent of all manufacturing are concentrated in forty metropolitan areas. The remaining 120 sizable cities contain only 16 per cent of the population and 19 per cent of the manufactur-ing facilities. In other words, we are so highly concentrated as to invite attack. If we had a national dispersal policy, we could use the internal migration of population and industry (which go on anyway) to change this pattern fairly rapidly and with a minimum of cost and dislocation. If we had only had such a policy during the past ten years we might by now be in a position to survive even a massive attack. The next ten years offer an equal opportunity. But we will have to do more about dispersal than we have done so far—which is chiefly to discuss it.

A HAVE-NOT COUNTRY

In international economics America has almost adjusted to the unfamiliar role of richest nation. During the past ten years we have successfully made the shift from debtor to creditor policies. But now, as the preceding Chapter tried to show, we have to make an even greater one—from having enjoyed in all our history a raw-materials surplus, we will come to the new experience of a raw-materials shortage, becoming for the first time a "have-not" nation. The much-publicized dollar gap, the chronic and apparently incurable shortage of dollars in the outside world, may well be replaced by a shortage of foreign currency in American hands to cover the purchases we want to make abroad. America's economic health will increasingly depend on our ability to export enough manufactured goods to pay for our import needs.

Two conclusions follow that at first sight may appear both paradoxical and mutually exclusive. The first is that low American tariffs on manufactured goods are rapidly becoming obligatory. We are in a very exposed position precisely because of our high productivity. Every other country with a similar lead—France in the eighteenth century, Britain in the nineteenth—eventually became complacent; it is always harder to stay ahead than just to get ahead. And liberal tariff policy is the best—perhaps the only—safeguard of high productivity. Low tariffs are not primarily the means to live up to our obligations as world creditor and world leader. They are a domestic necessity, and are increasingly so recognized by many (though by no means by all) of our manufacturing industries. The fact that the low tariff fight is no longer led by Southern agrarians and New York bankers (the traditional free-trade groups) but by manufacturing leaders like Ford, Burroughs Adding Machine, and IBM is an indication of how drastically we have changed.

The second conclusion to be drawn from our becoming a "have-not" country is that we must lead in the rapid economic development of the underdeveloped areas in our own urgent self-interest.

We must conclude this book on America's domestic future in the recognition that events beyond this country's borders may play, whether we like it or not, the determining role. Not only does the shadow of atomic warfare darken all prediction, but even if we assume a relative amount of luck—immediate postponement of major conflict by fighting an indefinite number of little ones—we will have to recognize how many of our internal rewards depend on our international wisdom and leadership. In politics, as elsewhere, the two entwine—and offer the major parties a double opportunity to capture national leadership.

The demands that an expanding economy will make on public policy are clearly so great and so new that they will force drastic changes in political alignments, organizational structure, and voting patterns. Yet at the moment neither party seems adequate to the issues of tomorrow. The Republicans, with their vulnerability to futile nostalgia for a past that never was, and the Democrats, with their almost obsessive fear of depression unemployment, seem equally impervious to the future. Yet the very fact that the two congressional parties are so evenly balanced in popular appeal suggests that the first to produce imaginative, bold, and realistic economic leadership might thereby gain a twenty-year ascendancy.

But the same is true many times over of the demands—in fact, the absolute prerequisites—of our international position. Unless they are satisfied, none of the opportunities here sketched will ever see reality. And they can only be satisfied by a firm, determined, and long-sighted foreign policy—dedicated to the economic and social development, rapidly and peacefully, of the Free World. For the first time since the Louisiana Purchase and the War of 1812, that is, foreign affairs have returned to primacy in the national scene. This seems likely to be the most enduring fact—as it is certainly the most revolutionary one—of America's Next Twenty Years.

Set in Linotype Baskerville
Format by Norma Stahl
Manufactured by The Haddon Craftsmen, Inc.
Published by Harper & Brothers, New York